The Eternal Gospel

That which is called the Christian Religion existed among the Ancients, and never did not exist, from the beginning of the Human Race until Christ came in the flesh, at which time the true religion, which already existed, began to be called Christianity.

—Augustine, *Librum de vera religione,* Chapter 10

The
ETERNAL GOSPEL

By

GERALD HEARD

HARPER & BROTHERS, PUBLISHERS
New York and London

THE ETERNAL GOSPEL

Copyright, 1946, by Gerald Heard

PRINTED IN THE UNITED STATES OF AMERICA

G-W

To

C. W.

CONTENTS

INTRODUCTION

THE Trustees of the Ayer Foundation have this year invited a layman to lecture. The reason for doing so is, I judge, that, having had those already who could answer questions, they would now choose one to ask them: Having attended to experts with a message, they would now listen to a layman's queries, to which such a school as this may reply. Certainly my own justification for addressing such an audience is that I might possibly suggest problems for which the layman is seeking solutions.

I have accepted this position of questioner because I believe that today the intellectual climate is changing and that even the expert may gain something from the inquiries of the nonspecialist. In the natural sciences it is now being recognized[1] that expert analysis through an exhaustive critical technique is not the whole secret of productive research and discovery. It is in fact but half of it and the second half. Fruitful hypotheses are equally important. In the natural sciences this primary factor in research was forgotten. For the basic hypotheses—such as mechanism—had so long been taken for granted that they had come to be regarded no longer as hypotheses—i.e., inventions of the human mind. They were assumed to be Natural Laws, objective and unvarying facts of the outer universe. Indeed it is now confessed that facts do not of

[1] See Woodger, *The Philosophy of Biology.*

themselves assemble themselves into Laws and that a subject may remain in a most unscientific condition of incomprehensibility and, indeed, confusion, not because facts are hard to seek. On the contrary, the confusion can be due to an embarrassment of observations which conflict and refuse to be brought under any known "law." The subject then has to remain in suspense until some original mind can imagine a system in which the data would take order. It is also confessed that the type of mind which can order the material is not the type called critical. A brilliant prosecuting attorney is seldom a creative artist. It has been suggested, therefore, that every research school should have two types of specialists. The high critical faculty must be maintained but, in order that these acids may have something to work upon, there must also be "hypothecators," men whose one task is to suggest themes of research for others to prove or disprove. How this might work, how "hunch" or integral thought might be organized, will be suggested in the lectures that follow. All that I would say here is that I look upon the position in which you have done me the honor to place me, as some such office.

The epoch of basic questioning has again come round and the outsider is called in that he may ask again the primary questions. American religion, philosophy and culture have gone through as entire cycle of development. Beginning with the Pilgrim Fathers, who migrated bodily but stood fast spiritually, the movement accelerated with the balanced progress of the sages of Concord, and has ended in our day in the meteoric flight of Permanent Prosperity. Spiritually the American Odyssey may be described in its three stages as Puritanism, Deism and Ph.D.-ism. The first was religion, the second was culture and the third is civilized chaos, a Babel wherein every year a new sector of workers ceases to understand the language of its neighbors, a deluge in which the inundation of information is supposed to be raising a new continent of knowledge, but is really submerging the last archipelagoes of understanding. No wonder the Tower is always subsiding and the flood washes us away.

I do not, however, believe that this state of things need continue. Our civilization is not foundering, it is capsizing: that is quite a different thing. For the vessel can be righted. Our disbalanced development is the cause of our distress. Our obsession with physical-mechanic means has given us power without purpose. If, however, we employ the same amount of attention to understanding our end, the meaning of our lives, we shall recover. The question I would raise is precisely that: Is not this generation one of unique opportunity for religion, if only religion can realize the size of that offer? As Dr. Inge has said, "Nothing fails like success," and the very opportunity which physics and economics have given, has proved their one-sided inadequacy. The men of action know that they must be given a psychological and spiritual knowledge equal to, contemporary with their physical knowledge which has gotten out of hand. They cannot produce it themselves. That is the province of religion. But religion can only produce this essential knowledge if it is contemporary. The Laws of the Eternal Gospel are of their nature unchanging but each generation must make its own contact with these Laws. The Laws of outer Nature were as much *there* for primitive man as they are there for scientists today. The triumphs of science lie in explication and application. I would ask, Is not that our situation, our challenge and our task in religion today?

[xi]

"Who is able for such things?" we may cry with St. Paul. But we may remember his balancing exclamation, "Woe is me if I preach not the Gospel." It certainly is not for me to preach to you. My task is to inquire of you how the needs of modern man—of all of us—for a rebalanced life might be met by a restatement in modern terms of those Eternal Laws, which because they, and they alone, bring peace to men of good will are called the Eternal Gospel, the Perennial Wisdom and Good News.

PART I

"As It Was in the Beginning"

I

What Is the Eternal Gospel?

THESE lectures will probably raise two provocative questions in your mind at the start. In the first place, What is the Eternal Gospel and, secondly, Why should Christianity contribute to it? I must, then, define my terms before asking you to consider my proposals. "The Eternal Gospel" is a phrase which has had a peculiar and not very creditable history in the apocalyptic corner of Christian theology. The phrase flickers for a moment on the confused background of that particular Apocalypse which the Church chose to canonize, and, from that phrase that curious and influential author, Joachim of Floris, in the twelfth century built up his system, his interpretation of history, past, present and future. This system, though temerarious, was itself never condemned by the Curia. But in the hands of the Rigorist Franciscans it was a thorn in the side of the Papacy and a place of departure for theories which were not less resented by the secular powers.

But, now that this withered tree is given over to the antiquarian historian, behind all the topical controversy, I feel we can discern in Abbot Joachim's theory of an Eternal Gospel something far larger than a medieval protest against the Church's complacent secularism and blind traditionalism. His philosophy is in germ a philosophy of history and, had he been able to carry it to its logical

[3]

conclusion, he would have found himself back with the younger Augustine, whose theory of religion I have used as motto for these lectures. Yes, he would have gone even further, to the fresh young shoots of Christian thought, and, leaving the already toughening climate of Carthage, have come to that earlier, far more creative world of the Alexandrine Fathers, who spoke openly and enthusiastically of the "Christians before Christ." Joachim's theory of history saw the story of man in three stages. The first was "of the Father," of the Letter, of the Law. Its binding virtue is obedience. That is all that is required of man at that level. The second was "of the Son." At that stage there is added knowledge "by reading." What we might call information, argument and critical analytical understanding is added to tradition and explicates authority. The third stage was "of the Spirit," and its characteristics are "prayer and song," meditation and inspiration, or, as we might say, using Professor Radakrishnan's term, integral thought, that intuition which apprehends the essential in the accidental and the eternal in the temporal. Joachim, naturally, saw this stage in terms of the vehicles known to him and his contemporaries. It would then be an age when contemplation would triumph, contemplation which gives that direct experience of spiritual reality which therefore can supersede tradition and authority. But it is clear that what he means is what a modern theologian, Dr. Inge, has called the promise and hope of our age, the exchange of the religion of authority for that of experience.

Joachim's vague but embracing insight on man's story had to wait some four centuries before it could be made more definite. It was another southern Italian, Vico of Naples, who was to carry forward the philosophy of his-

[4]

tory—a man far more remarkable than that greatly over-rated modern, Spengler. Our concern with these pioneer attempts to see humanity's epic whole, is with two specific points: First and foremost in the thought of these men there is present, if latent, the idea that as all history is one, so all religion is one also and in religion is the secret of man as a social being. The Eternal Gospel has always been known to all mankind, though with varying explicitness and though, of course, man has been free to disregard that knowledge. It is that mysterious Social Heredity that has made out of an animal, which had been deprived of all its specific instincts, a human being who can by his moral code, his categorical imperatives, preserve his sanity, his society and his survival. Secondly, the historical story is a vast spiral. Man begins in an implicit tradition, an unwritten Law, an atmosphere of social suggestion; he passes into a middle term of analytic, specifically rational and individualized knowledge; and he finally emerges into a state of intuitional thought, direct apprehension. This picture is, of course, one of an evolving consciousness. Emphatically it is not one that would attempt to explain the human process in economic terms. To that position I believe we have returned today.

We might use as a synonym, then, for the Eternal Gospel that phrase now popularized by Dr. Coomaraswamy and Mr. Aldous Huxley, the Perennial Philosophy. But I feel that the Perennial Philosophy is only part, a cross section of the Eternal Gospel. The Perennial Philosophy is, as it were, the actual Canon of Scripture (in many tongues and from thousands of years) in which, during that age which Abbot Joachim called "the age of reading," the Eternal Gospel was crystallized in written words. I hope, however, to show that Joachim is right. Before that age of the Scriptures, there is the age of traditional obedience, "of the Father," as he called it. That is the age before argument—still less apologetics. For the first commandment in its original form is undoubtedly, "This do!" "And thou shalt live," is a later gloss added by the age of the persuasive word.

I would then define the Eternal Gospel by a double phrase. It is, on the one hand, that essential sense of obligation and intuitional moral knowledge which has emerged and become defined as the common denominator and working factor in all the great religions. On the other hand, it is that element owing to which those religions are great and enduring. Of course we can, if we wish, use the phrase, the Perennial Philosophy, for the whole process, in its three great epochs. For Sophia in its original sense is a skill whereby a man becomes competent to express an art. It is not wisdom in an academic sense, meaning the capaciousness of our memory and the competence of our critical apparatus. It is the insight whereby a man understands the nature of the material in which he works and can produce, therefore, practical results. Philosophy in this deep original sense is, then, not a professional knowledge of systems of thought but rather the proved capacity to be an artist in creative living. So, too, the Eternal Gospel is not a series of dogmas or schemes of salvation but is rather that praxis and training by means of which the individual man becomes whole, through which he learns who he is and what he may become and the place and possibilities of himself and his society and mankind.

But when it is said, as above, that the Eternal Gospel is the working factor in all great religions and also that it is owing to this factor that they are great, I would guard against any appearance of a defensive circular argumentation. You will recall how, when the two young Romantic poets tried to corner that survivor from the Age of Reason, the literary critic and banker Samuel Rogers, he escaped their toils. "What is your religion?" they asked: a question always awkward and at that time far overstepping the limits of delicacy or indeed decency. Rogers evaded with, "The religion of every sensible man," and when the pursuers asked, "What is that?" he escaped into the impenetrable defense: "That is what every sensible man keeps to himself."

When, then, I say "great religions" I mean those religions which have over a wide area and for a couple of millennia (since the rise of religious individualism) satisfied the highest demands of the human conscience, intellectual as well as moral. Of those highest religions I would give as illustrations Christianity, Brahmanism, Buddhism and Taoism. The common highest factor may be found present in the three aspects of a religion, viz., its cosmology, the ethic it deduces from that cosmology and the psychology which this ethic and cosmology are found to indicate. The cosmology I would call High Animism. If Animism is a dubious word then I would use the term "Atmanism." It is as much above Anthropomorphism, as early Anthropomorphism was above the Low Animism which it superseded. High Animism is that religious philosophy or theology wherein the notion that the world is governed (or misgoverned) by a number of arbitrary individuals, "men writ large," a polytheism of anthropomorphs, becomes morally reprehensible and observationally false. The moral requirement makes such men postulate a Lawgiver, one and just: the factual observation shows that such Law does exist: Law is a single principle and it is just; sparing, and indeed guiding, those who keep

[7]

it, regardless who they may be and punishing those who defy it. I am aware that at times the actual expression of the Law and the law giver are identified but, I would ask, in those cases has not, then, one or the other of two things taken place? Either the Law is preserved from becoming a blind, unconscious Law by being held as a Living Law,[1] in which case the Law so seen is that Principle which reveals all that we, as we are, may know of Life and Creativity, otherwise beyond our comprehension. Or the Law *does* become blind and unconscious, and then there results an arid predestinationism which outrages morality and ends in mechanism which denies any objectivity to ethics.[2]

In those religions (Brahmanism and Christianity) where theological speculation is permitted to use vernacular, rather than technical, terminology, we may add to the definition "High Animism" the further term "Trinitarianism." Beside declaring that there is an all-pervading Power Who manifests His presence by Law, a Being Who if we cannot yet know His nature we may begin to learn how He functions toward us, two of the highest religions develop a Trinitarian doctrine. They use it, in Brahmanism under the titles of Brahma, Vishnu and Rudra, later Shiva: in Christianity the Father, Son and Holy Ghost, to define further the Essential One's process of acting on creation. He creates, sustains and completely resolves. A very important emphasis is, of course, placed by Christian theology on the central term so that the parallelism between Vishnu

[1] Such would have seemed to have been the attitude of later Judaism under the influence of the Chassidim and such, the Pali Text Society seems to suggest, was the attitude of primitive Buddhism toward the Dharma, a Living Law of Enlightenment, an Inner Light (cf. "Thy Law is a Lamp unto my feet").
[2] But see further ch. x.

and the Logos is less obvious than between the Christian and Hindu concepts of the Creator. But we must remind ourselves that that parallelism is there. Not only is Vishnu the preserver and so the constant repairer, redeemer, restorer; Vishnu is that aspect of the Trinity that incarnates, Krishna the Good Shepherd of Hinduism being the fourth incarnation of Vishnu. Nevertheless, as I hope to point out later, Christianity in its great emphasis on the Second Person of the Trinity and his specific redemptive activity, is making perhaps its most important and certainly its most constructive contribution to the Perennial Philosophy. We may add that whereas in the later Hinduism, which replaced the figure of Rudra by the Chthonic fertility figure of Shiva, the emphasis on the completing work of the Third Person seems to become almost destructive rather than integral, in Christianity the Paraclete, as the Lord and Giver of Life, is certainly that inspiring Power that raises the redeemed and salvaged creation to something higher than a mere restoration. Again, this is a question to be left till later, but we may ask, here, whether in these two differing interpretations, there may not be disclosed a difference of attitude not so much ethical as one of ultimate speculation?

Hinduism, it would seem, is inclined (as indeed was Augustine's metaphysical master Plotinus) to consider the whole temporal process as a tragedy resolved by Salvation. Where Christian theology emphasized the Paraclete doctrine, it teaches that the time process, in spite of all the mistakes possible and actual in it, is not an aberration or lapse but an Eternal gain.[3] This "Paraclete" view is more

[3] Nicholas Berdyaev has said that in the mystic development, as taught by the Orthodox Church, the stage known in the West as the Great Desolation or Dereliction does not occur and he suggests that

[9]

difficult: it easily involves itself in metaphysical stalemates. But that does not mean that it is wrong. We may, for a long while, be compelled to give wrong reasons for right things; for the simplest explanation is far from being invariably the most accurate, and in psychology it would often seem that the Law of Parsimony is a far poorer guide than it is in physics.

The ethic deduced from such a cosmology may perhaps, then, be rendered in two terms: Sacramentalism and Charitism. Sacramentalism is a vague term but it is the most convenient expression to describe that attitude which man as an individual should take toward social recognition, economic possession and physical appetite. Utilitarian hedonism also attempts to make life worth living to a creature who needs to be socially popular, economically solvent and sensually comfortable, by advising the satisfaction of each of these demands in so far as it will not interfere with the others. It proposes a balance and a difficult one. Indeed so much do these three claimants on man's service demand, that many have maintained that balance among them is impossible. If you would have the approval of your community you must balk your appetites. Nay you must—as the community's most praised activity, war, shows—you must endure hardships which make the phrase "the Right to Happiness" ring completely false. Even he who would be rich must generally choose between wealth and health and, in any community other than a

---

this may be specifically due to the fact that in the Greek Church the doctrine of the Holy Spirit is emphasized far more than in Catholic Teaching. Certainly an exclusive concentration on Sin and Salvation, as can be seen in certain aspects of St. Paul's teaching (e.g., "the vile body") and more so in Augustine's, tends to consider the whole physical creation as "fallen."

plutocracy, he must face considerable social odium if he would dare succeed beyond the moderate standards of good taste. Hence we see in history a continual reaction from the exasperating labor involved in trying to meet the exacting demands of that triad of suppositional blessedness: health, wealth and happiness. Men seek refuge from this triangular torture of Tantalus. For it is a torture. Here are its mutually exclusive claims: You must be popular, so be recklessly brave and generous. You must be wealthy, so be first out of any failing enterprise. Keep the rest out of anything that is prospering, and sleep with one eye open. You must be healthy, so avoid strain, live comfortably. Let Rockefeller have his dyspepsia and the heroes their hernias.

"No," says the observer, "it can't be done, any more than the circle can be squared." Very well, then; the whole thing is a fraud and a trap. We take refuge in "life-rejection." Every historian is aware with what relief men at certain times of reaction, for example at the outbreak of that religious pandemic usually called Franciscanism, have embraced poverty, chastity and anonymity. But "life-rejection" and "life-acceptance," in spite of Dr. Schweitzer's and others' support of such a dualism, do not exhaust the possibilities of practical philosophy. H. G. Wells once remarked after considerable reflection on biology and history: "The mind of the universe can count above Two," and Hegel, though now unpopular, does with his Triad present us with at least one further alternative. The Perennial Philosophy, I suggest, teaches, as a deduction from its cosmology, an ethic which does not say that life is itself good or in itself evil. Life is neither to be blindly accepted nor rejected. For life is a means, not an end. Life is supremely important and precious, provided you know what

[11]

to do with it. It is, therefore, with that proviso, very good; provided meaning is what gives life value to you and provided you can find that meaning and live up to it. An egg is a good thing provided it has not been kept too long. Few things are so bad as an egg that has fallen behind.

As illustrations, therefore, of the Perennial Philosophy on the basic issue of ethics I would quote two great source thinkers: The first stands at the beginning of our Western science: the proto-Hellenic philosopher Heraclitus. His apothegm, "Here we are as it were in an egg," declares that we are a transitional creature, a creature whose life and health depend on its moving at a certain critical velocity. He complemented this insight with his further direction: "The senses are bad witnesses." The implications of that we must leave for the moment. We can find a confirmation of his estimate of the human situation in that beautiful phrase carved by Akbar over the gate of the city which he deserted as soon as it was built, "Said Jesus, may his name be blessed, This world is a bridge, pass over it, but build no house upon it!" That the ethic of the Perennial Philosophy finds authentic expression in specifically Indian thought can be seen in the well-known saying of Sankara, "Give thanks always for having been granted a human body," for a body and that place which it gives in the world are the *sine qua non* for achieving the knowledge of God.

When, then, I suggest that the ethic of the Perennial Philosophy, the rule of the Eternal Gospel, is Sacramentalism, I am using that phrase to express what might be called a dynamic asceticism. But this spiritual athleticism is sane and saliently balanced, because its chief aim is not to render itself either invulnerable, the danger of Stoical ἀπάθεια, or in a state of arrested healthiness. Sacramental-

[12]

ism neither rejects life, still less calls it an evil, nor accepts
life as having adequate meaning in itself. Every experience
can be useful: no experience, whether sensation, action or
thought, can be final. Hence appetite, possession, recognition, the physical, economic and social requirements of
the individual are lawful and right provided they are used
as means, not conceived as ends. As Augustine has said,
these things are dangerous and will become evil provided
we cease to use them as means and look upon them as ends
—as things to be enjoyed in themselves. They are necessary
means to our one true end and only possible happiness:
the knowledge and contemplation of Him Who has created
us, so that we may only find our rest and completion
in Him.

Further, we may say of Sacramentalism that, as it looks
upon appetite, possession and recognition as necessary
means to that growth of spirit, that evolution of consciousness, which is our *raison d'être* in this space-time world,
so it is always socially minded, essentially ethical. The
problem of individualistic ethics, so poignantly, indeed
almost grotesquely put by Kant, that true altruistic action
really means doing good to someone I dislike, because if
I do good to those I like how can I be really altruistic, here
is solved. I can be happy, only provided I act in a social
way. In sacramental marriage passion amalgamated with
tenderness gains the power of lastingness which alone can
satisfy a creature that must otherwise be tortured by regret
and pity. In co-operative enterprise the power to accumu-
late generates resources which permit further creation.
In creative appreciation, in constructive criticism a truly
organic society gives to those who express its ideas that
challenging inspiration to do better, without which the

[13]

greatest genius must become either slack or capricious, complacent or idiosyncratic.

Such in brief definition is the Sacramental aspect of the Perennial Philosophy's ethic. Sacramentalism is that attitude of mind which keeps a man awake and alert, mobilized and ready to deal with the incessant contingencies of life. In this spirit he cannot only make his appraisals of what is being offered him so that he recognizes the true nature of each experience and is not taken in by appearances. He realizes that this life is a test, and he is being judged that he may show not so much his intelligence quotient but his understanding quotient, his U.Q. rather than his I.Q. But he must do more if he would really be educated by living. His detached interest must not only watch the event but also his own reaction to that event. He must inhibit in order to study and understand. "Man," says Rousseau—no friend to self-control—"man only thinks when he is prevented from acting." The life-deniers say, mortify your impulses. The life-affirmers urge we should get rid of repression and let life have its head. The Perennial Philosophy would teach us never to do anything without at least striving to understand why we are doing it, to strive to see whether it is part of a complete co-ordinating purpose. This canon of behavior is taught in that illuminating incident given in the Codex Bezae where Christ, seeing a man working on the Sabbath, only but wholly remarks, "If thou knowest what thou art doing blessed art thou, but if thou knowest not what thou art doing thou art cursed." To this training, in self-understanding and growth in power to comprehend life's meaning, is added its complement, charity. I have used the more definable word "charitism" because *caritas* is more than almsgiving or the power to speak kindly. Charitism is an

[14]

attitude toward all other creatures, an attitude which intellectually, emotionally and volitionally recognizes that the neighbor is oneself or, in the more comprehensive Sanskrit phrase, *tat tvan asi*.

The psychology which such a cosmology and ethic would seem to indicate, brings us to Heraclitus' second apothegm: "The senses are bad witnesses." Taken with the first saying, "Here we are as it were in an egg," we have defined an important finding of the Perennial Philosophy. Again it rejects either extreme. Those "idealistic" philosophies which maintain that the apparent world of phenomena is *Maya* or *Lila*—an illusion or a byplay—are, I would propose, as aberrant as those which maintain materialism. This experience which we are undergoing in the body is not only relatively real, it is of far greater significance than any Humanistic materialist can ever rate it. Actually it is not an illusion. As far as we can tell it is a selection made by our sense organs from certain bands and wave lengths of vibration, and those selections are combined so as to give us the impression of a colored, sounding, sensory world. By skilled cross-examination of our senses we can discover and have discovered not only that they respond to but a very small part of the vast volume of potential stimuli which are presented to us, but that out of the selection which our "set" is at present attuned to pick up, we make a construction which is certainly not the only one possible. Few lines of research will yield, I believe, more important results for human understanding and happiness than those which already have yielded confirmatory evidence of Heraclitus' insight, that the human postnatal life is an embryonic growth in consciousness, of the psyche, as the prenatal life is a fetal growth in physique. Again we see the central and balanced position of the Perennial

Philosophy, avoiding the extreme, on the one hand, of saying we should get out of the body as soon as possible, or, on the other, that we should stay in it as long as possible. As there is a critical velocity of growth at which the embryonic physique must elaborate until it is ready for birth, so there is a growth velocity at which our consciousness should evolve. The eight to nine months of the physical fetal life may be matched by the eight to nine hundred months of the postnatal life.

In a phrase, then, the psychology of the Perennial Philosophy is one which sees consciousness as something that evolves. First identified with its body, as that body was at the beginning of growth identified with the body of its mother, this consciousness gradually distinguishes itself from its encasement; until—final analogue—it discards that protection which has become a limitation, beginning a form of life under utterly different conditions of function and apprehension. The body is therefore neither the end of man nor his obstacle. It is the womb of the soul.

Such, then, I would venture to believe is the Perennial Philosophy, the Everlasting Gospel. If I may summarize its main features they are these: Denying both materialism and extreme philosophic idealism, which must end in solipsism, it maintains that what we are undergoing is a very real and supremely important experience. It is true that we do very largely construct the world which we call objective but that construction, if we understand that it is a provisional and transitory construction, is as useful as a pontoon bridge to a traveler crossing a river or a shell to the hatching chick. Further, if we so understand that our consciousness is a moving and growing thing, we can make larger constructions to house a wider apprehension.

> Till we at length are free
> Leaving our outworn shell by life's unresting sea.

Thirdly, as we are a psychic embryo, as each individual is an evolving consciousness and that is the meaning of life for man, that evolution will only continue if that unit of consciousness wishes to evolve. Conscious evolution can only be done consciously. Man must then decide by repeated and sustained acts of will to stretch out to larger unperceived apprehensions. Fourthly, such a creative reaching out requires two things: (1) a letting go of, or piercing through, superficial findings, limited ends, the restricted goals of appetite, possession and recognition, a penetrating down and into ever deeper and more comprehensive bases; and (2) a deliberate operational acceptance of relationships to which the emotions may, at first, only give a negative response. The morality of the Perennial Philosophy is summarized in the two commandments, unlimited devotion to the supreme Reality and a strenuous denial of any interest which would in any way deflect or restrict that devotion, and the determination of the creative will to regard all creatures as children of that All-Father.

II

The Stone Age Eden

I HAVE now made two proposals in regard to the Perennial Philosophy: The first is that it has specific characteristics of cosmology, ethic and psychology, that it holds a central position between those two aberrants, the This-life-denying philosophies and the This-life-affirming ones. It says, This life is good, if you know enough to understand what this life is good for. It maintains that this life is good but not good enough by itself. The Ever-lasting Gospel is a *via media* but it is not vague. It is polar to sentimental humanitarian optimism.

The second proposal made about this Philosophy of Life is that it is a development, a condensation and in the end a "classic definition."

How then may we call it Perennial? This is so vital a question—as vital to Christianity as it is to the Everlasting Gospel—that we must take some little time to define the situation.

It is often said today that Christianity is a historical religion. It is important that we should acknowledge this. Indeed, as I shall suggest later, I believe we have only begun to realize what that statement involves. The old prehistorical, or pre-anthropological notion that you had only to dig back to primitive sources to find the religion that would suit our contemporary world, scholarship has compelled both Protestant and Catholic to abandon. But, further, if we stress, with a sense of worth, Christianity's historicity, we must not deny the historical element in the whole process of religion. We might say that religion is a process of a constantly extending balance. It is that maintenance of identity with an ever-expanding change, which is the outstanding and mysterious characteristic of life itself.

The Perennial Philosophy is, then, in essence eternal—it is the unchanging Law of man's nature. Its expression, however, changes, as man's power of expressing himself and defining his circumstances both grow in precision. We should then expect to find that the Everlasting Gospel should have gone through a series of defining steps. What was latent from the beginning had to be made successively explicit.

As such a conception involves our current notions of progress, we had better first examine how those notions appear in the light of this conception of history. First, however, we should define the term "progress." It is so popularly and so loosely used that few people now remember that the man who did so much to make it current—the sociologist Herbert Spencer—picked such a phrase precisely for its moral neutrality—its freedom from any reference to values. Progress meant simply progression or process, when the term was originally used by the nineteenth-century social thinkers, who were working with the evidence of physical evolution and then extrapolating such biological lines of development out into human history. Herbert Spencer has said that he did not wish to involve himself in discussions as to human betterment and so selected a term mathematical and not moral. It was not a sociologist but a poet who wrote:

> .... An increasing purpose runs,
> And the thoughts of men are widened with the circling
> of the suns.

A poet who managed to combine genius with financial, familial and social success and who, therefore, may have been prejudiced in thinking that things were getting better, at least for poets.

Professor Bury has shown in his *Idea of Progress* how the whole notion of human improvement is a modern idea and only popularized by the end of the nineteenth century. Progress therefore means, if precisely defined, just what Herbert Spencer said, a process of development from the simple to the complex, and, we may add, from the diffused to the defined. We can add still further, as our anthropological knowledge has grown, that as the development has become increasingly complex, it has required increasing balance. As man's evolution goes on he does not by mere growth become better and find himself automatically a higher moral being. There is no evidence of this, and, if there were, it would be a grave obstacle to a moral view of life. For it would mean that we ourselves have to make far less moral effort than our ancestors. And in the end the whole effort of the past would have the crowning frustration of having produced a generation in which at last any moral effort was absurd. What actually happens is that in each generation there are born fresh minds of indefinite adaptability in order that these may have the creative task of answering in new terms the unchanging Interrogations put to them and the whole race.

If, then, we accept the evolutionary hypothesis, we may say that if man is derived from an animal, up to the close of his animal evolution his progress is a unison—that is to say, his physique and his psyche are one; what the creature desires, that is racially right it should desire; what it wishes to do, that its physique both makes possible and is itself developed and preserved by the doing.

During that huge hyphen of history, those five hundred thousand years and more that lie between animal man and civilized man, during the whole span of the paleolithic cultures, man becomes a tool-using creature. During that phase the first great division takes place in man's nature; he becomes double natured. Unconscious, psychophysical processes still grow his physique, and by no taking of thought can he add a cubit to his stature. But another process is adding to his reach. By a skill, so slowly acquired that it takes one hundred thousand years to alter the way of edging an ax, man is developing a method of working which lies halfway between instinct and invention. So man is growing in two directions. He goes on growing physiologically (though there is evidence to show that he does not *evolve* physiologically any more), and he begins to grow those extensions of his limbs—tools. His inborn physiological heredity, generation after generation, gives rise to the same type of body. But a new and far more flexible thing, a social heredity, is now giving rise to a new succession, a series of types of tools.

All this may seem a far cry from religion; but it is not. And only if we understand how the roots of religion are already present at that level can we hope to understand its fruits today. This matter of social heredity is of primary importance. For social heredity means two possible things. In the first place, it means that as man now has a double nature, a physical nature and a mental nature, conflict may arise between them. To take the simplest possible ex-ample: a Chellean man, a man of the first phase of the

[21]

paleolithic cultures (if we leave Eolithic man still in a suspense account) faced with a fighting stag, might, in his excitement, forget to use his stone club, and, trying to pull down the buck with his naked hands, be gored to death. The danger of "throw backs" in behavior is henceforward a possible risk.

Secondly, and though this is not so evident it is as certain and no less significant, man's social heredity is itself a double thing, or of two aspects: it has a side which is expansionist and that we see clearly—we see the tools steadily, if slowly, improving in design and multiplying into special sorts. But man's social heredity has another aspect which balances his expansion that would otherwise be disruptive; that other side is the power of cohesion. During that epoch of five hundred thousand years which we are now considering—the hyphen between animal evolution and deliberate invention—these two aspects, of expansion and cohesion, had not come apart. Studies of such Stone Age cultures, as the Arunta tribe in Australia still maintained when Spencer and Gillen visited them, show that societies at this level certainly do not analyze a proposition as we do. To them the modern idea of efficiency, of an object being made simply that it may perform one particular physical purpose (a use to which its massproducing maker may himself actually never put it), is an inconceivable notion. There is no necessity that we should accept the suggestive, if temerarious, notions of Levy Bruhl or Durkheim about *le participation mystique* and the prelogical mentality, if we do allow that the paleolithic mind has a different notion of time from ours. Means and ends are not separate things. Hence when an object is being wrought one of the purposes of so working is, it is true, to have in the end an object which is an effective economic instrument. But the object is more a precipitation of a process than a deliberately envisaged goal. It is quite as important, if the flint toolmaking is to be "good," that the right song should be sung, the right rhythm of strokes struck, the right chorus chanted by the onlookers, as that the actual knapper should know where and how to flake. A group ritual is performed and one of the end products is a flint ax, another, and quite as important a product, is a renewed sense of social solidarity.

Thus we see an early simple authentic form of Sacramentalism. So we see economics and psychology, science and religion in reciprocity and balance. We also see why any attempt to add to economic efficiency is generally at the cost of psychological value. We may add that such an attempt to increase economic efficiency regardless of the possible loss of psychological worth is probably a symptom of some fissure in the consciousness of the individual who so plans. A blind area is forming in his mind, a blind area of which he is unaware because of his increasing absorption with a hypnotizing spotlight of interest, interest in getting tools which will give him greater material gain, absorption in the outer world.

What is undeniable is that such developments toward efficiency and specialization do go on at increasing pace, toward increasing complexity. We may also add with a fair degree of certainty that in spite of the strains which such expansion must have caused to primitive man's social structure, that structure seems to have weathered those stresses.

What made this advance possible? How was man able to increase the economic efficiency of his instruments without disturbing that psychological value which had been so largely present in the old way of making them? If he were to increase means, and increasingly to aim solely at increasing means, how was he to prevent his ends from shrinking until his only goal was economic efficiency?

The answer would seem to lie in man being able to make a corresponding advance toward understanding what Kant called the Realm of Ends. Prior to this stage, failure by a man to accord with the Law of Life left no alternative but his elimination—death. The vitality to make the right response was inadequate. With this stage an alternative appears. Three courses are henceforth possible: to live well, to die, to live ill, as all parasites live, a death-in-life. It is here, in fact, that we first come across what may be specifically called religion. Up till then, till specialization of function appears in man's instruments, I believe we may think that he made no recognized distinction between process and end product, between the psychologically rich ritual of procedure and the object which resulted from such a rite. Now, however, he is compelled to recognize that the process has two aspects—one that satisfies his psychosocial need of a sense of group solidarity—a communion of activity—and another that goes on and permits him to satisfy his economic need, his need to have, through improving instruments, a greater power over his environment.

This crisis is of particular importance for two reasons: In the first place, here we come upon that "horizon" when man's intelligence rose above an undifferentiated, unreflective behavior pattern which satisfied his feelings and resulted in a certain economic advantage, and began to differentiate between ends and means. The second consideration is more important to us, though less emphasized by paleoanthropologists. It is that man achieved that advance, he secured the advantage of greater economic efficiency, because he was able to make a corresponding advance, a balanced extension of invention, in his psychology. It is here that we come upon a principle of cardinal importance to mankind. I would indeed say that on our ability to recognize this principle and to act upon it, rests our entire future. It may be put in a phrase: Every advance in economic and physical discovery, every further definition of efficiency, every invention of means, must be balanced by an equal discovery and definition of ends. We may put it another way and say: Every time man believes he has further understood his environment, and by that understanding can manipulate it and exploit it more fully to his physical advantage, it is vitally necessary that he make a corresponding and balancing further understanding of his own nature, of its entire demands and of how those requirements of his whole nature may be met and not infringed, how his nature may be preserved from being fractured and may continue its growth entire.

I believe it is of great importance to recognize that with man's development of a variety of tools for special purposes, with the emergence of Neoanthropic man in the Aurignacian and Magdalenian periods, man also gives evidence of specifically psychological inventions. It is from this epoch that we have those amazing eidetic cave paintings. Into their representational mastery this is not the place to go. What we have to note is their psychological significance. I can only mention three points with the utmost brevity: First, the only human figure shown is that of a dancing man dressed up to represent a composite beast, half stag, half carnivore. (This is the so-called Wizard from the Grotto of the Three Brothers.) Secondly, the vast majority of the figures are drawn over and over again on the same ground and following the same strokes. (We may compare this with the persistent repainting of the great Greek icons.) Thirdly, these pictures are almost invariably in the total dark of the innermost cave, only to be seen and only to be drawn by lamplight. Those who have studied these works with anthropological and psychological insight have become convinced that here is evidence of a mind that, realizing its need to identify itself with ranges of life from which it found its own intelligence rendering it increasingly alien, has invented a process whereby that identification may be repeatedly re-established. In the dark, lit only by the wavering flicker of a small oil lamp, the artist saw in the looming shadow of the rock boss, the humped shoulders of the bison, the heaped neck muscles of the lion and the boar. His relationship with these creatures—and he drew others such as the grasshopper which must have been of no economic value—he established psychologically here in the deep dark of the cave, in the sanctuary which lay behind the dwelling section which gave on the outer air and light. Beside these repeated drawings we have also man's first musical instruments, of stone. And in that invaluable relic, the subterranean cave under the hill on which stands the castle of Montespan, we have the model of the cave bear in the midst of the main hall and, still impressed in the area around it on the mud floor, the prints of the dancing feet that trod that sacramental measure perhaps twenty-five thousand years ago.

Here then we have actual evidence of a *religio*, a rite of unification, of communion, of a whole corpus of psychological inventions, ritually repeated drawings, music of a definite scale, ritual dance. And these psychological definitions and exemplifications are not merely to give to the tribe a new and more vivid sense of its own unity, a unity which the dawn of analytic method in economic crafts might well call in question, but also meet its spiritual need for a sense of identification with that vaster outer nature which otherwise will become wholly alien, something merely to be dreaded or exploited.

Into the immensely important question of totemism and the part which it plays in all Sacramentalism I must not go—not even to ask a few questions. I hope to do that when we are considering this new knowledge (for there has been a revolution in our notion as to what totemism actually is) in the light of Christianity's teaching in regard to the redemptive process.

Before, however, we leave this too brief consideration of the dawn of specific religion, I would ask again: Is not its importance to us that it shows that an advance in physics, in physical invention, must be matched by a corresponding and balancing advance in psychics: that any definition of a process, so that it may serve more efficiently an economic aim, requires an equal definition of that part of the original process which served a psychological need? Probably no part of a primitive process is useless. What part we have called useless is that aspect of it which originally met a spiritual requirement. Man cannot live simply by efficiency because man does not live by bread alone. Furthermore, do we not see in that vast hyphen of history—the history of paleolithic man—how true progress may be made and in what true progress consists? "God made man upright but he sought out many inventions," sighed the weary writer of the Book of Wisdom. Should we not say, "Inventions must needs come but woe to that man or society which invents more power and fails to discover correspondence of purpose, who explores and

[27]

conquers the outer nature but who fails to explore and unify the inner nature"?

. One might suggest the main theme of history to be this: That man, as he rose from the animal level, had to grow in what I would call "detached consciousness." I call human consciousness "detached consciousness" because I believe it is a grave mistake to call it, as we usually do, self-consciousness. Generally self-consciousness is that particular development of consciousness which is positively morbid. I am aware that it is popular today to label general states of mind by their extravagant and morbid manifestations. That charming and valuable type of person who is vivacious and enterprising and who corrects his ebullience by moments of a not less appealing discouragement as to his own rightness, we dub one of the manic depressives. While his counterpart who is quiet in his advances and endures his defeats in silence we say is a most promising case of schizophrenia. To be conscious of the self is, then, not an extension of consciousness but rather a contraction. That we assert when we say, "I was so self-conscious I could not hear what was being said to me." An additional reason why we should call human consciousness detached consciousness is that, as seen in the study of the psychology of wild animals, what we call, rather loosely, "instinct" is attached consciousness: the animal pays persistent attention only to those things which serve its physical appetites or its racial requirements. As soon as these needs are met, the object of interest, or even of devotion, such as the young of birds and mammals, is treated with indifference and, should the object continue to solicit care, with hostility. Man, and man alone, of all the creatures, can and does pay persistent attention to a vast range of objects from which he is detached, because toward them he can

[28]

make no reaction with his body, and from them he can gain no satisfaction for his appetites. This development of consciousness is then a true evolution, a rightful advance. It carries with it, however, the risk of degeneracy. The wild animal is held on the rails of instinct. Its conscious wishes and its physical and racial needs are not in conflict; it therefore keeps willingly the Law of its Being. Man, however, when he is permitted to emerge into detached consciousness, is free to choose to what he will attend. And the supreme danger is precisely this: that man may and can and does choose not to attend to a larger range of interests than those which serve his health and the forwarding of his race. He chooses to attend to something smaller, he chooses to be narrower and more selfish than any animal can be, to be more exclusive and less wise than the blindest instinct. He chooses to attend to himself, not even to the needs of his physique, not even to the health demands of his body, but simply to such restricted and perverted sensations as may reach that strangulated foreconsciousness which he calls his ego. Egotism is the auto-eroticism of the psyche.

So considering history as a development of human consciousness, as a shadow cast by the growing mind of man, we can see the truth in the dictum of the *Theologia Germanica*, "Nothing burns in Hell save the Self." We can also see (as will be developed later) the significance of the Hebraic-Christian theory of the Fall. It seems inescapable that there must have been some period in the full cycle of human history when man, possessed of the power of detachment and free to disobey nature, used his powerful freedom not to integrate himself with a larger purpose and greater understanding. He might have gone on, freed from racial subjectivism to see the world from the Cre-

[29]

ator's standpoint, Whose service is perfect freedom. He chose to secede, to become only fully aware of his egotistic self, and of anything else only in regard to himself. His appetites, his possessions and his position he would use, only and wholly for his private egotistic enjoyment and indulgence.

The penalty was, of course, not a geographical banishment from a physical Eden. It was banishment from his own inner unity and balanced understanding. Till then means and ends, urges and satisfactions, powers and meaning, value and reality advance in unison and may be sustained in an expanding harmony. Every development in efficiency gives, not merely more economic power, but the process also yields a further possibility of enrichment and exemplification of the social pattern, and clarity of understanding in the human outlook. The primitive pack is happy doing things together. But it hardly knows that it is happy, scarcely is aware of its communion, unless the group is divided and some are banished. The organicized human society with each enrichment, becomes increasingly aware of its happiness. Conversely, as soon as this social enrichment is neglected, as soon as any physical and economic advance and invention is not matched by a corresponding and balancing psychosocial and spiritual invention, man's interior disbalance, his increase of restless egotism, develops and his social cohesion correspondingly wanes.

It is this process of social degeneracy by increasing fissure in human consciousness, that we can trace in early religion. And here I would say that a principle already recognized in physical evolution becomes in turn apparent in psychical evolution. That principle is illustrated by the fact that all forms, when they are losing their power of

[30]

development and so becoming decadent, tend to produce massive rigid structures. Hence it is far easier to study decadencies and aberrations than the forms which were the actual carriers and vehicles of evolution. Indeed, as we know, nearly all the fossil skulls of hominid creatures were at their finding thought to be, because of their massivity, ancestral to Neoanthropic man, and are now thought to be, instead, aberrants. So, too, with religion, we have tended to think, because brutalized forms have lasted on, or left convincingly forbidding traces, that primitive religion was base. We must also remember that the true apostolic succession leaves little trace. We can gauge its path by the silt of superstition that, on either side of its clear swift course, gathered and remains, while the spirit went on its way bearing inspiration to each generation.

We can assume that through the long hyphen of history —the five hundred thousand years of the Paleolithic— man's specific development of social pattern grew with each development of his physical inventiveness. Dance and rhythmic representational drawing and music—these specific social inventions we see developed *pari passu* with his equipments of tools and crafts. And further we see this development not only keeps him united with his group, not only guards him from the illusion that because he can make economic discoveries therefore he is an ego which is only tied by an economic nexus of personal physical advantage to his group. The rite which reunites him with his group also gives him, in contemporary explicit terms, in terms as definite as his consciousness has become defined, the knowledge that he is one with all life and with the whole of nature. To be definite at the risk of over-precision, I would then venture to say that the Fall, the

[31]

fractioning of man's consciousness, of his nature into two parts and his alienation from his sense of unity, did not take place when man rose from the animal level and became a toolmaker and fire tamer. There was a time when man was innocent of the sin of secession, of the wish to be separate, and that point was not at the animal level. It was not, I believe, that in becoming man that man fell, but after he had achieved, or been raised to manhood, when he chose to misuse the powers newly acquired. The Fall we would be wise to hypothecate as coming *after* that long epoch of his life as an organized hunter. It occurred when he had entered on the agricultural phase of his history. That may be the explanation of the story that Cain the agriculturist kills Abel his flock-tending brother.

Certainly we may assume that there was an epoch of Animism. By that I mean a period during which man was aware of his fellows, of wild life and of all nature as being part of an all-pervasive Life, when he was aware of this supremely important psychological fact *with a similar degree and level of definition* with which he was aware of the physical factuality of his tools, of their purposes and process and of the material world on which he exercised them. It is that fact that I would emphasize. Neither his science of toolmaking nor his metaphysic of the soul is the explicit science and metaphysic which our contemporary individualized analytic mind must use. But neither is his reaction to his fellows, to other life and to "inanimate nature" any longer the reaction of an animal, any more than his economic methods are those of an animal. He does not worship anthropomorphic or theriomorphic gods, but he already worships; and he is worshiping Life, the Eternal Life which has created him, sustains him, restores

[32]

him (in dance and ritual meal and totem rite) and which receives him back into Itself.[1]

I would, therefore, combine and enlarge Tylor's title, Animism, with Otto's phrase, the Numinous, to furnish a label to this important phase of man's life. That phase begins when he successfully emerged from animal level and began his mastery of his environment by invention, and yet achieved this great and dangerous increase in outward power without deranging his inner balance. This was possible because he was able to make psychological inventions which, though rudimentary and hardly explicit, nevertheless were as explicit, as "scientific" as the physical inventions which he was making at that time.

But it may be asked, Is not this Low Animism? I would say No. It is Primitive Animism but it is uncorrupt and so able to give rise in due time to High Animism. It only becomes Low Animism when with it there enters the idea of magic, the fancy, prompted by the ego, that the Eternal Life is merely a reservoir of force and may therefore be coerced to serve the ego's physical desires.

This, too, may be the place to point out that as Primitive Animism could and probably did suffer from the decadent development which we call magic, so, in turn, when man reaches the stage at which his psychic evolution makes him think of all consciousness as fully individualistic, this anthropomorphic stage can have, at its level, a right aspect and a wrong. It is then that we get the defined conception of gods and devils; and in devil worship, under which category we must include all worship that regards the deity as cruel and requiring cruel sacrifices, we have the specific aberration of the Eternal Gospel.

[1] The burial procedure as disclosed by the Mount Carmel burials of a Neanderthaloid species of man.

A real progression of dynamic balances then was possible to man. But the price of liberty is always vigilance. Every increase in power and means calls for an increase in purpose and meaning. If physical inventions are to be constantly increased then psychical inventions must keep pace or the ship of man's advance will capsize. The activity of that aspect of man's consciousness which thinks continually about mastery of the outer world must be balanced by an equal activity of that aspect of his consciousness which is always aware of his relationship with "the beyond which is within." We can say, with a high degree of assurance, that this exacting balanced advance was not sustained and it is therefore at that point that I would place the historic Fall; or, to put it in our psychological vernacular, I would say that it was at this stage that there took place that fissure between the conscious objective mind and the subconscious subjective mind, that aspect of the inner-looking mind which henceforward was to be repressed and lapse into what we now call the subjective mind. A primal unified mind, a mind neither analytically scientific in its physical inventions nor artistically conventional (hieratic) in its social devices and psycho-spiritual methods, broke in two. The "lever" aspect of the mind was reared up into a state of unrestrained critical analysis, in the belief that by resolving everything into ultimate inert elements, man could raise himself above all accident, while the "fulcrum" aspect of his mind foundered. It is at this level of his development that man, owing to this fissure, becomes unaware that the mental interior world is as extensive, as unknown and can need as much control as the outer world. Man's ignorance of himself grows, then, *pari passu* with his absorption in the outer world. And, of course, this "outer" world is not "objective," for it is and

[34]

can be no more than the abstraction and interpretation made by the five senses, which five senses the ego now assumes to be the only and wholly valid describers of reality.

Of this fact, that an advance in practical physics nearly always means retardation, and even arrest and retreat in true psychology, we have three clear pieces of historical evidence. The first derives from religion itself, in the degeneracy of the Life Religion. The Numinous Animism becomes contracted and corrupted, shrunken and defiled into a Fertility Religion which becomes in time specifically phallic. The second piece of evidence is the division of religion into Olympian and Chthonic, religions of bargain or of fear, *do ut des* or *do ut abias*, white or black magic. The third is the emergence of conflict in the individual, in the community and between mankind, exhibited specifically by psychosis, criminality and war.

The responsibility for this collapse must, I believe, be laid at the door of religious practitioners. As Lawrence Lowell used to say, "No country has ever been murdered: they all have committed suicide." That is certainly as true of religions. The practical man's mind is absorbed in what he takes to be the outer world, for the practical man is not a realist or an analyst and therefore identifies himself with his senses. But if the deeper thinkers work as hard at their level as he works on his superficial areas, he will not be contemptuous of them. On the contrary, the more efficient he is the more he is aware of depths which he cannot plumb and, as in his own province he works by empirical methods and specialization, the less is he inclined to dismiss as fanciful those findings given him by experts who do produce results. It is then not religion that has failed practical man and which that man despises, but fraudulent religion. The point where religion became fraudulent and corrupt was when the priesthood, the specialists whose task it was to keep religious knowledge contemporaneous with physical and economic knowledge, failed, by greed and sloth. The tragedy of religion may perhaps be put in the phrase: The price of open vision is perpetual self-sacrifice and, finding that price too high, rather than pay the cost of winning actual contemporary experience the religious fell back on tradition. The men who were advancing knowledge of the outer world were continually testing and ever more searchingly experimenting, adding to past findings, correcting and enlarging old findings. Verily they had and have their reward. The men of inner knowledge, however, degenerated into drones. They wished more and more to find their satisfaction in sharing in the increasing economic plenty which the outer discoveries and inventions were winning. They declined to make researches in their own field. They neither gave the psychological value for the economic benefit given them, nor did they themselves in their own sphere find even for themselves further satisfaction. They were official artists who had ceased to cherish any love of art. They had sunk to being academicians who only cared for the money profit of selling pictures, which were bored and slavish copies of a lost vision. They no longer believed even themselves, what they, at best, were now teaching at second and, maybe, at hundredth hand.

Here then we may perhaps detect a second Fall. The first Fall was when man's mind broke into a foreconscious ego which could only apprehend the world through the five senses. This second Fracture-Fall, this next psychological "faulting," was when man's social heredity fissured, when sensory analytical knowledge went on to become physical science, when psychological integral knowledge was not equally pursued and religion accordingly became superstition.

It is very important to realize here that religion, when it falls into this condition, does not simply become traditional, ankylosed, fossilized. It is not an atrophied limb: it is diseased and corrupting. For the process of mental detachment, of psychological contraction of focus, of individualization and analysis, goes on inevitably in every individual throughout society. Indeed it goes on more quickly among those in the more advanced and influential positions. Therefore this process, which is the mental side of evolutionary development and not under the control of the conscious individual, must be present among the religious just as much as among the secular. Man, whether he be priest or practical naturalist researcher, has no choice in this respect. His consciousness must grow in detachment, in critical awareness. The primal undifferentiated awareness must divide in two—growth must needs come. Man's mind must cease being monocular and become binocular; there is no necessary Fall in that. The choice, always offered, is whether these two, the inner and the outer aspects, shall advance in balanced reciprocation or whether these two shall fall apart and one side, the analytic side absorbed with the outer world, shall proceed alone. Then it will try to control both fields of experience, the inner and the outer world, and will attempt to force the inner aspect of apprehension, the power of what now must be integral thought, into subconsciousness. And here we must again remind ourselves that primitive pre-egotized man has not a subconscious mind any more than he has a foreconscious analytic mind. The primal consciousness is a "fluid plastic" out of which the "solid state of mind" and

[37]

the "liquid" have *both* to be formed by separation from the primal amalgam or "magma."

This description of the process is not speculation, a deduction from what may well be called psychological embryology. It is established by historical evidence. For we can see that there comes a time when man's power of analysis so rapidly increases that while his physical powers multiply with unprecedented rapidity, his capacity to make a co-ordinated social response is failing. We see unmistakable signs of the emergence of oppression, tyranny and warfare. And when we examine the religion that is contemporary with this decadent period we find in it similar evidence. The priesthood was itself individualized. It had not made the effort to keep spiritual experience contemporary. That would have required experiencing in the comparatively modernized consciousness of Bronze Age man that awareness of the Eternal Life which had been experienced by paleolithic man at his level of more diffused consciousness. But the priesthood at such an epoch (*circa* the Bronze Age) could not be self-consciously cynical. Two steps had to be taken to reach that goal. The religious who were proving traitors to religion could not arrest analysis, for analysis, we have seen, is a symptom of the inevitable growth of consciousness. Therefore, as they would not be loyal to the growing life of religion, they had no choice but to analyze in physical rationalistic terms what had been a psychological integral experience.

Hence the Life Religion, the general sense of the Numinous, contracted and degenerated into the specific Fertility Religion, phallic worship, and, when the phallic worship as a specific form was suppressed, into the blood sacrifice and human sacrifice.

Nor is that all. The phallic and blood sacrifice stages of

[38]

decadent religion are not merely stupid and depraved. They are certainly, in some aspects, as actively morbid and destructive as the bloody violence of the new killer, the soldier. The psychological conflict which at that date is causing struggles between tribes (the dawn of warfare) is also splitting each tribe itself. The priest and the warrior are now engaged in thinly-veiled civil war, each attempting with his specific force to forge a weapon to destroy the other. We see the growing physical violence of the "extroverted" met by corresponding cunning on the part of the "introverted." Physical cruelty is being countered and increased by those mental assaults and tortures which we include under the name of witchcraft.

Into the complex richness of the second phase of religion there is here no room to go. All we can say is that it is aberrant and decadent and is due to the failure of the priesthood to keep psychological knowledge abreast of physical knowledge, to preserve that balanced advance whereby the increasing detachment of man's consciousness (which had turned his economic intuitive gestures and activities into clearly understood and definitely aimed skills and crafts), should correspondingly develop his psychological intuitive gestures (dance, chant and rhythmic drawing), into clearly understood and definitely aimed spiritual exercises and acts of established communion with his fellows and with the whole of life.

The Perennial Philosophy has no part in this failure. Unfortunately, our attention is more easily arrested by tragedy and catastrophe than by successful persistence. Especially in a romantic age does religion tend to be melodramatic. Our time, because it believes that there is no meaning in the whole, tries to make man's defiance of the cosmic process the center of attention and the climax of

[39]

historic action. We have thought that the phallic and blood religion were both primitive and comprehensive. They are neither. The actual line, the only true apostolic succession, is as difficult to trace as that actual ancestry whereby man rose from animal to human station. The giant wrecks of false deviations leave vast fossil remains. The spirit not only blows as it lists; even when it incarnates, it uses the frailest of vehicles and so leaves little trace of itself. Because an ill-running engine makes more noise, because morbid hypertrophy arrests the eye, we can watch man, and hear his cries of passionate self-pity, as he pursues his outward unbalanced course, running into increasing difficulties in which his increasing powers only involve him more deeply in unbalanced conflicts. He is already set upon that aberrant line of advance in which means will increasingly be enlarged and relied upon, first to solve all the problems of ends and finally to be a substitute for ends.

This phase of history is now generally recognized and named as the Heroic Age. Vico was the first historian to detect it, to recognize that behind what till then had been called barbarism there lay a pre-barbaric age. Chadwick in his lucid summary, *The Heroic Age*,[2] showed, what anthropology has increasingly confirmed, that the Heroic Age has its specific, and very unstable, psychology. It is a type of consciousness which marks a violent reaction, a fear-response, to a collapse. That collapse was of the old religion which had degenerated, by the contraction of diffused consciousness, intellectually into magic, emotionally into eroticism. The Heroic Age, whether it be illustrated by the character of Abimelech in the Book of Judges, Achilles in the *Iliad* or by the asuras in the Vedic

[2] See also Dr. Harold Peake, *The Bronze Age and the Keltic World*.

epics, is an age of protest. We have been, alternately, impressed by its courage, enterprise and fine phrases and repelled by its violence, its disregard for thought and compassion, its false simplification of life's subtle difficulty, its childish assumption that the long involved knots of society can be cut by the sword and that all problems are merely material, to be solved by an unreflective courage. The driving force in today's totalitarianism is the spirit of the Heroic Age reborn, disguised as an engineer. Our task is neither to condemn nor to admire but to interpret that age. We must see what caused this unbalanced outbreak. It is the obvious and epicentral disturbance caused by a seismic subsidence and factioning in the foundations of man's mind. The fissure of his consciousness, long subjected to intense tectonic stress, at last takes place with cataclysmic suddenness.

The priesthood's interpretation of religion at such a juncture could no longer be tolerated. It was obviously both disgusting and untrue, and, in the few cases where magic power worked, it proved to be antisocial and horrible. Magic was an attempt to render in terms of self-centered individualized consciousness, absorbed with the material world, the old animistic generalized reactions of the preindividualized tribe.

The man of action broke with this revolting sham. What authority had Micah the priest over Abimelech the gangster? None. And a few generations later we see Saul, the typical "hero-king," not only breaks with Samuel the numinous prophet-judge but he also attempts to exterminate the witch cult. Hence it seems to the author of that almost unexpurgated document of the Bronze Age, the Book of Judges, "Every man did what was right in his own eyes," for, "There was no open vision." The pessimistic

[41]

author or editor is right in his conclusion. He is not quite accurate in his premise. The Heroic Age is not quite morally lawless. True, there is very little contemporary experiential religion. But tradition is still able to prevent complete anarchy. For example, the sex taboos of Heroic barbarism (to call this individualized kinesthetic culture by a balanced term) are very strict. For this culture is a reaction from the licentious ritual of the Fertility Religion. Nor is the fear of bloodguiltiness absent. The fall of "Homeric" Troy, to take an instance, was dated by classic writers and, we have found, dated accurately, by the fact that the home town of Ajax Telamon sent until Roman times a reparation team of men and women at regular periods to give free labor to the Troy district. This reparation was rendered because Ajax at the sack of Troy rushed into the city's temple and killed Polyxena, daughter of Hecuba, who was kneeling there. This sinful disregard of the Law of Sanctuary, Ajax' own swift death by drowning could not discharge. His town for centuries had to shoulder the guilt. Such was the conscience of a barbaric age. We can hardly imagine our civilization taking so seriously blood-guiltiness for the death of the innocent.

The killing of anyone actually associated with religion was a deed from which these toughs shrank and if a herald were killed or wounded terrible consequences befell him who had so sinned. To plumb, but not to exaggerate, the depth of the collapse, we may say that religion, which had sunken intellectually to magic and emotionally to the orgy, naturally could no longer control men possessed by a new, acute sense of their individualism, a sense which made them both destructively critical of authority's magic claims and also indignantly disgusted by its orgiastic practices. For we must remember that when the threshold rises

[42]

between the conscious and the subconscious, the primal consciousness is sundered. This means that man becomes, simultaneously, nonsuggestible, that is, incapable of accepting the dogmas of tradition; and also, as he becomes alienated from his social heredity, he becomes alienated from his own primal consciousness and disgusted therefore by sex.

Add to these two facts, that men had become nonsuggestible and sexually repressed, the fact that their individualized mind, becoming egotized, pushes on to economic efficiency and to the invention of new weapons, and it is obvious that an Age of Disorder was inevitable.[3]

The second fact that makes us able to view the conclusion of the Book of Judges as too despairing a picture is that though open vision was probably lacking and seership had little inhibitory power, yet it was continuing.

It is this thin line that we must now trace in order that we may watch the Law in men's hearts growing in clarity and definition, so that it may match and balance the grown definiteness, the increasing Law-fulness, of their knowledge of the world of the senses.

[3] The invention of iron weapons (*circa* tenth century) in the Caucasus, gave, as Peake has pointed out (*op. cit.*), rise to a series of horde wars. Cf. the Cimmerian darkness.

III

The Fall and the Sphinx's Questions

I F MAN'S history is the shadow cast by his growing spirit then we may say that we have reached, in this our sketch, that moment when that shadow suddenly took on an unprecedented definition.

We have traced with the utmost brevity that vast epoch during which man can satisfy his speculation with the conviction that he lives in a universe that is somehow alive with the life which he feels in himself. To cover that, under one title, there has been used here a psychological extension of the term Animism, a term which Tylor coined to denote man's religion in what used to be called its pre-anthropomorphic phase. But today anthropomorphism cannot be considered as an adequate definition of post-animistic religion. For anthropomorphism is not the actual definition into which Animism contracted. When man could feel no longer the general undefined sense of the Eternal Life round him, or recover it by the monthly Life Festival, his religion ceased to be the Life Religion and specified and falsely contracted into the Fertility Religion. The Fertility Religion is not anthropomorphic but phallic. Sex, not life, is now worshiped. Contact with the life consciousness is now made, not by the group dance and sacred meal, but, as the difficulty in making that contact increases, it is attempted by sexual orgy or alcoholic intoxication.

There follows an attempt to recover from such a false emphasis and mistaken definition; and the outward sign of this is the destruction of the phallus and phallic images (such as Hezekiah's destruction of the golden ophic phallus and the stone testes worshiped up till then in the Jerusalem temple), and, in the stead of this, the worship of the sun or entire athletic human forms.[1] Man is thereby attempting to regeneralize, but he does not go far enough. By his destruction of the phallic religion he has suppressed sex and, with it, the whole of the intuitive side of life. This is shown by the two facts: (1) that the anthropomorphic gods are "Olympian," sky gods, day deities; and (2) that the gods who had been fertility deities, of the darkly pregnant earth, become denigrated, gods of the night and of evil. This is very clearly shown in the two figures of Hecate and her terrible daughter Proserpine, who later, through the Eleusinian mysteries, are brought back as goddesses of redemption from death.

Man has then hidden, choked and lost the deep wells of his own intuitive knowledge of his unity with all life and therefore with his own Eternal Life. But he has not gone on and come to perceive the demonstrably working Law in the world around him. The anthropomorphic gods are neither potent nor lawful. They are arbitrary creatures of no value. They may be made respectable but they cannot make others holy. For they are projections of that very temporary phase in man's history when he thought himself to be only and wholly an individual. Anthropomorphism seemed to early archaeologists to be, first, the primitive religion and, then, typical religion, because prepsychological archaeology first caught sight of those figures which

[1] See Dr. Samuel Henry Hooke on the phase of sun worship in Hebrew religion.

[45]

best lent themselves to sculpture and so naturally stood up vividly against that dark background of Animism, where imagery is little needed, is mainly symbolic and nonrepresentational.

Indeed it may be doubted whether any really religious man ever believed in an anthropomorphic polytheism. The whole of anthropomorphism may be no more than the representationalist artist's attempt to render an experience of which he only knew by hearsay. Here, then, we should have one more illustration of the fact that we have found and will find all along: the statuary, furniture and temples, the outward rites and organization, are never the actual traces of those contemporary manifestations of the Eternal Gospel. They are, rather, the silt and precipitation left on its banks and thrown aside, like the moraines on either side of the rock-scoring glacier.

The real and right step in religion which man made when he emerged from Animism and had to define his relation with the Numinous, was, then, neither the error of phallicism nor the mistaken correction of anthropomorphism. It was the discovery of Law, of Natural Law in its two hemispheres of moral and physical Law. We can see why anthropomorphism is a mistaken correction when we view it in its most favorable light. Low anthropomorphism is obviously contemptible. The contempt which dismisses all religion as a vulgar and ignorant projection of man's own passions, caprices and fears, makes its case from low anthropomorphism. But high anthropomorphism is more dangerous to real religion, because its mistake is subtle and deceives even the good. High anthropomorphism does conceive of moral law, but because it makes a distinction between the law and the lawgiver, it ends by making moral law less real than physical law.

It would seem that there was a time—a passing epoch—when man so thought of physical law that cataclysms in outer nature were caused, not by law in that realm, but had been set in motion by an anthropomorphic deity who was vexed by man's behavior.

However, when men recognized causality in the physical world they saw that there was no caprice in consequences. At once it was clear to them that there was help and strength in the recognition of physical law because physical law is self-sanctioning. But as long as men think of Deity as anthropomorphic they will never get rid of this limitation, that the universe is not self-sactioning, in regard to moral law. They cannot but think of moral law as something more shadowy than physical law because moral law, it is imagined, does not carry its own fulfillment in itself. Because of this an external humanoid deity seems to be needed to enforce it by irruptions into the physical realm. To such thinkers a cataclysm is only an unpleasant miracle.

We must, however, here guard our thinking. Men often cling to anthropomorphic notions of God because they believe the only alternative to be a dead, rigid Law, a blind necessitarianism. That, too, is a false projection or extrapolation. What actual observation has established is that we find ourselves in a world of lawful freedom. As a man sows, so shall he reap. But not only is he free to sow; he is also free to learn, from mistaken sowing, how to sow rightly. His mistakes are not irretrievable but educative. His errors are not fatal punishments, not threats but warnings. Man has learned and does learn by doing wrong and by acknowledging it. To condense the argument in a technical phrase: There is no evidence of iron necessitarianism, or rigid causality in nature. It has never been found and, according to Heisenberg's Principle of Indeterminacy, never will. What has been found is the Law of statistical probability and on that have been built all the triumphs of ordered foresight in regard to nature, while within that frame of working there is also guaranteed freedom for the individual man. If we were told to devise a world in which conscious creatures should be able to learn by experience; in which they should find themselves, not in a capricious environment but one which was regular, reliable, manageable, where what you did led to foreseeable results; and, meanwhile, in that environment there should be these conscious creatures, given intelligence so to understand their setting, given memory to recall their successes and failures and free will to act on these reflections, neither bound by fate nor given capricious power to escape consequences: would we not create just such a world and such a human species as we now find?

I do not say whether it is likely or unlikely that such a world should exist. All one must say is that in point of fact it does exist, and that any attempt to make out, either, that it is capricious (anthropomorphism) or necessitarian (mechanomorphism) is untrue to the facts of observation. That anthropomorphism and mechanomorphism both make a world in which a moral being cannot function or grow is a second consideration. Conversely, if anyone thinks that it is strangely and arrestingly apt that the physical universe should be found so to be the environment in which moral development could best take place— that the Law of High Numbers and the Indeterminacy of Low Numbers together make precisely the condition required for spiritual education—he may well discern here an argument which could reintroduce Natural Theology.

[48]

For is there not valid evidence herein for a God-made world?

But whether that be so or not, the fact remains that we are in such a world and that we are ourselves such creatures. We have then to conclude that we are not faced and controlled by a dead and rigid necessitarianism but by a Living Law. God is neither outside His Law nor bound helplessly by it. These are the typical false dilemmas of anthropomorphism. God is manifested to us by this Living Law which is, because it is an aspect of His Being, an educative Law, a Law of Life, the complementary hemisphere of that Law-fulness which we see explaining to us the otherwise confused manifold of the physical world. And we shall see further that, as we keep that Law in its two sides, we shall increasingly perceive two things: First, that moral law, when the essentials of that law are cleared of the local accidents (taboos, etc.) with which anthropomorphism encrusts it, is assuredly as self-sanctioning as physical law. The implications of this, for moral action, we must consider later: they are great. Secondly, we see that man's spiritual progress is thus along a knife-edge between an arbitrary anthropomorphism that may be swayed by gifts or sacrifices from its purposes, and a legalism that is so rigid that it may never be deflected. Mercy and Justice must be kept as a single term with these two aspects. Man has to walk the thin line between belief in a personal Deity so Law-less that all moral effort is otiose and belief in deified laws so inflexible that all moral effort is unavailing.

We cannot trace even in outline the fascinating story of man's wavering course along this line. We know that in Akhenaton's reign in the fifteenth century B.C. in Egypt the principle of Law began to emerge under the guise of

[49]

the worship of the undeflectable path of the sun. We know this religious reform broke with, and attempted to destroy, the Fertility Religion; that it suppressed sex and shut down the passage between the conscious and the unconscious mind. We know that the failure to answer man's question, "Who am I; whence come I; whither do I go?" made Akhenaton's reform worthless. He could and did destroy the sexualized Fertility Religion. His substitute died with him. The conservatives, however, as indeed is not uncommon, learned their lesson. The reformed orthodoxy with its significant symbol of Amon-Ra (the fertility Ram Amon with the sun Ra between its horns) gave a respectable exoteric religion to the masses and an effective esoteric religion, the Mysteries, to those individuals prepared to understand that the Eternal Life which the Amon-Ra promised was not merely the physical continuation of the race but the survival of death by the Eternal consciousness behind each individual ego.

We see here another grave difficulty that has till late interfered with our tracing the actual course of the Eternal Gospel. "Those who say don't know and those who know don't (or can't) say," is Lao-tzu's epigram in which he states the teasing paradox. Certainly those who least define what they do are most effective at doing, and their exoteric formulae (or dogmas) are least logically defensible. The conservatives, using external rites (which can be rationally disproved by those first rationalists, the prophets), are wrong in their reasons but succeed often in their praxis, for they are actually re-contacting the subconscious. The prophets are right in their reasons, their arguments and their demands, but they fail because they lack a praxis, a psychological technique. We must always remember (for here lies the source of the conflict between the intuitionist

[50]

and the rationalist analyzer) that giving a wrong reason for an effective practice does not disprove the practice. As Aldous Huxley has said in *The Art of Seeing*, J. S. Bach would certainly have given a wrong theory had he tried to explain the physiological activity necessary for the fingering of a fugue, but, as certainly, his actual skill in fingering utterly surpassed that of any present professor of physiology. Further, we find, time and again, that while the theory may be demonstrably untrue (compare the Eleusinian ritual *et. al.*), or deliberately misleading, as in the astrological-alchemical disguise for psychophysical exercises (compare Hermetic, Kabbalic, etc.), or put in a series of arresting paradoxes (the Taoist scriptures, especially the *Tao Tê Ching* and the *Zen Kohans*) the actual praxis is kept concealed from all save initiates.

It is out of this turmoil—Bacchic: Cybelean: Orphic: Pythagorean—that there emerges the full conception of the Living Law—e.g., the emphasis put in Pythagoreanism on mathematics—the discovery that man has within himself a Law of his being which can be studied as objectively as the law of motion in the outer world. This Law is not alien but only hidden: it is not in conflict with his good but only with his wayward aberrant consciousness which has become self-absorbed. Find this and man will know himself. Man will be happy then as he alone can be happy because he will cease to be in conflict with himself, with his neighbor and with life. That is why Rhys Davis, the Pali Buddhist scholar in his book, *Buddhism*, calls the eighth century B.C. the real datum line of our new era. For since then no step of equal span has been taken. From that period, down to the present, all people of that social heredity, all mankind but those tribes left isolated from the main social development, have been contained within

[51]

a common field of reference, between a common sky ceiling and sea level of probability.

The dawn, however, was slow. Certainly before the eighth century B.C. there existed in a number of civilizations a realization that Law was a concept which must be added to divinity if divinity, which had become anthropomorphic, was to be saved from becoming only "Man writ large," a capricious and arbitrary being. The conception in its rudimentary form can be seen in the specific literature of the Heroic-barbaric age, the saga-epic. Both Wotan and Zeus at certain crises, as in the doom of Baldur and that of Patroclus, discover that they can do nothing. Behind these flashing figures, projected from man's hope that the brave cannot really fail and that strong action in the outer world gives lasting victory, emerge the cold and dreadful images of the impassable Fates weaving by unchanging Law, by causality, what no courage nor skill may thwart or unweave.

Yet the discovery of Justice's Scales is itself a balanced discovery. To the lawless and willful it means Doom, something repellent and frightening to the most daring; for the "weird" is etymologically simply the "Weave of Destiny." To "dree one's weird" is simply to go the way the unseen Law will drive even the strongest. "Yet the strong man must go."

To those, however, who wanted to understand, and whose dread therefore was not of the inflexible but of the capricious, the discovery of Law is a deliverance. "This do and *thou shalt live*." The Law is no thwarting but a way through the jungle of arbitrary events. A law is, in nature, a discovery how to go along the path, in the current, that nature has set and on which man may be carried. It establishes a new covenant between Reality and man, offering

[52]

him a partnership if he will observe Its rules. It alone can give meaning to his experience.

Why we have failed to recognize this is due to two causes. In the first place, Law imposes a limitation upon fantasy, upon the willful dreaming of the magician, upon the willful behavior of the buccaneer. It calls for effort from the fantasist and for obedience from the willful. Both the decadent priest and the private individual dread it. In the second place, the specifically moral reformers, such as the Hebrew prophets, and to a certain extent Akhenaton before them, though they proclaimed moral law, dwelt too exclusively on law as morality. They sought the sanction of their law, not in the completed circle of law by showing that there is no break between natural law and moral law, but in the dictum that natural law is moral and moral law is natural, thus confusing the two. They made a particular Deity a supreme personal ruler and He it was who sanctioned moral law which otherwise they held would be sanctionless.

This, inevitably, had very serious consequences in the further development of religion and still causes much confusion in ethicoreligious thinking and action. Indeed it is almost impossible to trace with consistency the advance of the Eternal Gospel in its increasing definition, unless we examine this situation with care. The difficulty caused by this failure to realize the objectivity and self-sanctioning nature of moral law, becomes strikingly manifest when dealing with the specifically Christian contribution to the Perennial Philosophy.

If, then, an exclusive emphasis on law as morality, rather than on morality as part of law, was one of the limitations of the prophetic schools, we shall be able to understand more clearly the significance which the idea of Law really

[53]

held for the progress of religion viewed from the Greek rather than the Hebrew standpoint.

Judaism, we must never forget, took on its specific moralistic character when Israel as a nation had had to face the ruin of its nationalistic hopes. This means that the ethics increasingly became individualistic rather than social, a protest rather than a policy, a belief that the Law of moral right runs at variance with the actual destinies of nations. Judaism turns, from a belief that the righteous—those who serve the anthropomorphic Jahweh—must succeed here and now, to a violent reaction of despair which in apocalyptic language states the faith that God will destroy this order, in which righteousness can never grow, and, obliterating the rich, who are equated with the wicked, He will create a new world (see the supremely influential servant passage, Isaiah 53).

The Greek, the formative years of whose social heredity were less unhappy, was first a naturalist and then an ethicist. Hence when he began to conceive of law he rapidly recovered from the chill which the conception of fate gave the Heroic Age. Indeed one may say the frost of destiny only killed off those hot-blooded men of action while it stimulated the men of thought to new adventure in ideas. The Greek as a questioner found in the idea of law an instrument whereby he could probe the world around him. His reaction to the idea of causality is not a paralyzing sense of predestinating karma but rather the cry, Eureka: a way is found through the jungle of the manifold. Even when he fails, his language shows his undefeated power to inquire. His cry, "I have sinned," is not the despair of the hopeless convict caught by the implacable judge but the confession of failure in order to do better. *Hamartino* ("I have missed my mark") both honestly owns the blunder, and, just as frankly, believing the mistake to be a fault under his control, sets about improving aim, instrument and marksmanship. Such an attitude toward life, sees its own nature and the problems of that nature as part of the whole of nature and nature's mystery. The primal and characteristic Greek apothogems show this: "Man is the measure of all things," and "Know thyself and thou shalt know the universe." Morality must, therefore, be part of nature. There must be a natural theology, and, as the Stoics concluded, there must be a law of nature which man's nature wishes to keep and in keeping which he lives well and truly. But, conversely, that law is not a rigid code; it is not written by an anthropomorphic finger on stone tables. It can be found; but, also, it has to be found. It is found as all laws are found, by watching, by experiment, in short, by asking questions of nature.

Greek morality, or rather the way the Hellenic mind when it reached law level built up its critically expressed rendering of the Perennial Philosophy, is based on a series of investigations, or, in its earliest form, questions. All peoples state their problems first in fairy tales or myths. The Greek states the beginning of a lawful morality in the myth of Oedipus and the sphinx. Here the young hero climbing the mountain, finds barring his way up the precipitous path the monster who is half destroyer, half mother. He answers her questions, knowing that if he fails to do so she will kill him, but if he succeeds in answering she must destroy herself and leave his path open to the summit. The questions as they have come down to us have, it is clear, in spite of their distorted form, to do with the nature of man and specifically with the problem of life in regard to death.

This is a narrowing of the general inquiry and the full

[55]

challenge of life, to that one aspect of individual physical growth, age and death which absorbed later Greek thought. "What is Death?" is, it is true, one of the sphinx's questions. But the questions cover the whole of man's moral problem, physical, social, spiritual. To do that, they must be five in number. Five we find them in all those statements of Law which have come down to us from the proto-prophetic age. Why the universalism of these five requirements has not been recognized by historians of religion is because we have considered them rather as answers, rulings handed down to man, as rigid and final instructions given by an anthropomorphic deity. The Greek way of considering the numinous power in nature, as a power that asks questions rather than one that gives detailed commands, is both truer to our knowledge of nature and to our intuitions of deity. A code imposer is succeeded historically by the seer who makes his disciples answer themselves. Further, this Greek way, what we may call the naturalistic rather than the legalistic way, of approaching Reality and the attempt to understand it as Law-ful, has the additional advantage that all law, natural and moral, is seen as one. Further, as natural law is self-sanctioning and itself rewards and penalizes those who keep and those who break it, so, too, is moral law. Moral law, no more than physical law, requires an external anthropomorphic lawgiver to support it with extraneous losses and gains.

The Five Interrogations with which man finds himself confronted when he realizes the lawfilledness of all his experience, may be listed briefly. Running up from himself to his neighbor and back again, they are: "What is Sex?" "What is Property?" "What is Force?" "What is a Promise, or one's Word?" and "What is Death?"

Now that we have put them as questions which man

finds himself driven to ask, we can see two further points—one general and the other particular. The general fact is that these questions, being questions, permit of varying answers. To forestall our inquiry for the sake of clarity, we may say here that no less than three answers on three levels are permissible. The only impermissible answer is the answer of complete egotism. For egotism replies to all the Five Questions, "Nothing. They all mean ultimately nothing." Of sex, egotism says, "It is nothing but a private physical pleasure." Of property and money it says, "It is nothing but my private possession." Of force, "It is nothing but such violence as I may be able to apply to get my own way." Of a promise, "It is nothing but my private word, to be broken when it suits me." Of death, "It is the supreme and confirming nothing; for whether you live for others or for yourself makes in the end no difference. It will all be the same in a hundred years."

The three permissible levels of reply we may call the individualistic reply, the social reply and the spiritual or universal reply. As an example of the first, the individualistic reply, we may cite the Decalogue. Though it is well known, the Decalogue is not a good specimen of the spirituality of its age. Here again we come up against the difficulty which meets us when at any epoch we would describe that epoch's expression and definition of the Eternal Gospel. The more defined any expression is, the less likely it is to be expressive of the best and the most spiritual thought of the age. The Decalogue is too individualistic: the individual is always its problem, if not its concern. That men would want to serve the community because they find a fuller life in it than in themselves does not seem to occur to the lawgiver. This awoke no suspicion when anthropology was prepsychological. But now that we know that egotistic individualism is not primitive, not in the line of life's development but an aberration, we cannot suppose either that the Decalogue is primitive, or even the best moral example of its age.

We can, however, take it as an individualistically over-emphasized statement of man's answers to the Five Questions. When he has reached that stage of detached consciousness which permits him to have the first suspicion of the universe's lawfulness, but when his detached consciousness begins to contract into that ego-consciousness which inevitably projects an anthropomorphic God, this is the code he must utter. Half of it will be ethical but the first part has to be sanctions for that ethic. For the ethic is not, and cannot be conceived by an ego-consciousness, as self-sanctioning. The law is then inevitably a double system. Its specific morality—its ethic is fivefold—its structure is, however, tenfold. That is because this, the Decalogue system, is evidently framed by men who, as we saw when considering the prophetic age (prophet and lawgiver are at first allies against the ritualistic priest), are so absorbed with personal morality and its principles as to be uninterested in physical nature and its principles. The conflict of man and society is their concern: not the relation of society and nature. The power to detect law was confined to human relationships. Social cohesion was in itself no longer enough to prevent individuals breaking up society. Individuals must use physical force against their fellow members and an individual God must intervene with physical punishments. The main demand is therefore clear: law must have sanction; if not in itself, then through a law imposer. An ethic which does not depend on a cosmology is untrue just as the cosmology which does not result in an ethic is meaningless. This balance can only be solved when ethics is realized to be part of cosmology. The first five commandments of the Decalogue are thus the attempt to arrive at an imposed cosmology which will sanction the second five, the social Laws, and so preserve society. The code is, then, what we should expect of the Semitic social heredity, that heredity which differs from the Greek by its comparative indifference to nature, its absorption in the problems of personal contracts and a keen development of the ego concerned primarily not with understanding but with gain. The cosmological part of the Decalogue, the first five dogmas, also tells us much about the stage to which the psychology—the condensation of the consciousness—of its drafters had arrived.

Deity is condensed from a pervasive presence, from Animism to Anthropomorphism. Other Gods are allowed to exist. But Deity is nonidolatrous. Here is an advance that must soon make men perceive that a God who has no image, no form in which He may be confined, is all-pervading. The third commandment makes this advance inevitable. God is one and without form: but He is not vague and far-off like a high cloud. He is always present, immanently transcending any screen or barrier which may hope to exclude Him. He is the witness of every act however secret: He hears every time He is called or spoken of. We are on the threshold of the prayer which begins the Eucharist with the ascription, "To whom all hearts be open, all desires known, from whom no secrets are hid."

About these three commandments and their cosmological significance there is little doubt, and with them is completed the definition of Deity made by Heroic-prophetic man. This man has not only become an individual, and cut off from his integral consciousness, but he has begun to press on through the temporary anarchy such a

[59]

splitting of the psyche causes, to the recognition of order, if as yet only of external order, by the perception of Law.

The next two commandments are in fact hyphen commandments. If the first three give us a cosmology and the last five an ethic, the fourth and fifth give us a psychology, a praxis whereby we may be able to make what we believe will result in consistent action. Because they are psychological they were dismissed by prepsychological and pre-anthropological critics as purely topical features embedded in the general code. Eight and indeed nine of the rules apply to, and are found among, all peoples at that stage of post-Heroic culture, of an egotism that has to be brought to book, offered terms and told if the terms are not met then either society or the individual must be destroyed. The fourth, however, was said to be an exception. It could only be the odd birthmark of a conservative people, who, clinging to the primal lunar cycle (the dating by the month and not the year, when all other cultures went onto a solar calendar) still observed, with a taboo of arrested activity, the four phases of the moon. Is not Nil Gal, the female moon goddess of the proto-Sumerians, the first named deity that has been found? Did not the Semites take much of their culture from Sumeria? Did not the Jews cling to moon feasts until so late that this practice awoke the anger of the later prophets? Is not our Easter still a lunar feast?

All this is true. But it only illustrates a fact fully recognized by psychology: when a psychological process is present and works so powerfully and efficaciously that it can continue right through the limen, when the limen has divided off the surface mind from any direct knowledge of what the deep directive mind needs and does, then the surface mind, blind to the actual process, will rationalize whatever behavior the deep mind requires. The post-

[60]

Heroic Semite thinkers who defined and imposed the Sabbath no doubt defended their so doing by maintaining that they were religious conservatives clinging to the ancient religion. They maintained that the moon goddess of the night, reigning over the mysterious female cycle of reproduction, was the original and efficacious deity. Later, when God becomes the Father, not the Mother, the rationalizing explanation was offered that God finished creation in six days and rested—and so we should rest on the seventh. But what was the actual value of this arrest of activity one in seven days? Research in psychology has shown it clearly. One of the problems of research in hypnosis, one of the gravest limitations of hypnosis as a therapy, is the fortnightly cycle. Suggestion treatment can be given which will eliminate completely, sometimes at a single sitting, such severe addictions as morphinism and dipsomania. The addictions, however, so often reasserted themselves in full force that this was one of the chief reasons for the abandonment of hypnosis by therapists in Europe. And the date at which the addictions returned to the house out of which they had been cast was found so frequently to be a fortnight that much research was devoted to this cycle.[2] It was clear at once, that this was half the lunar cycle. The next step was to see that suggestive treatment should be deliberately extended to carry on over the gap. Finally it was found that lasting results could be achieved if once or twice during each fortnight a suggestive treatment was regularly taken.

The Decalogue, therefore, in the fourth commandment is giving a psychological praxis. This commandment begins, significantly, with the key word of all mental method, "Remember." We must recall that these instructions were

[2] See Hugh Wingfield, M.D., *Hypnosis*.

[61]

made by and for newly individualized men who wished to curb their incipient anarchy, who could not, however, believe any longer in phallic gods but who were beginning to believe in law. For one of the prime factors of being self-conscious is that our oncoming mood or passion does not obliterate wholly the former one; as we do remember, we can and do begin to see the connection of cause and effect. The advice is then quite clear, reasonable and generally effective: It says, For six days attend to that world presented to you by the five senses and which now seems to your ego-consciousness the world in which you really count. But on the seventh stay still. "Muddy water," said that great prophet of this method of recollection, Lao-tzu, "let stand will become clear." Wait on God, says the fourth commandment, for a whole day in every seven; if you do, you will find you will progress in keeping the whole law. Your personal passions and obsessions will abate, and as the flood subsides the ancient landmarks will reappear. The stress of your ego-physical desires are loosened, the strained social cohesion will regain its elasticity and grip.

The fifth commandment completes the sanction side of the Ten Words. A newly individualized society is a pioneer society, experimental, exploring, impatient of taboos. The past has been found wrong, badly wrong, so often in the things it promised and in those which it forbade. It has deceived the individual for its own good and given him reasons which he could disprove. Experiment, empiricism, science, law alone are to be trusted. What can be proved to be wrong and against our personal advantage, from that we will abstain. With regard to the rest, surely we are free? The fifth commandment says in brief: Not everything that is slow is wrong, for some laws, like some mills, grind slowly. You may have to live till you are old to see the working out of laws that work with a lag. Honor your parents: they may not know the newest tricks of the new crossbow you have invented and their advice may not be expressed in the smartest syllogisms. But living has taught them more about life than you can know till you are their age. Save yourself the bitter trouble of buying fresh and raw and sore all your experience. Honor them and your days will be longer than those of the cocksure who disregard the "imponderables."

Now, turning to the ethics this cosmology and psychology indicates, we see it is consistent, i.e., it is on the same mental horizon, it is the expression of the same stage in the evolution of man's consciousness. Man is in the immediately post-Heroic level of culture. The code is one of law, but of law in a rudimentary, prepsychological stage. It is a matter of inducing a number of individuals to deny their actual impulses sufficiently to make possible a social pattern. Society must only demand that minimum, else the individuals, or perhaps the constituent families will secede and the tribe will disappear. That society can offer benefits which the family itself cannot provide, still more, that, beyond mutual self-interest and economic increase, society could give individuals ends so satisfying that economic gain would gladly be sacrificed—these notions, we have seen, the Decalogue does not seem to entertain. Hence throughout, whether by threat or reward, the appeal is only to the individual and in terms of his individual benefit.

Further, all save the last commandment, which is clearly an addition, are prepsychological in another sense. Motive and state of mind are never considered. The act alone counts. You may "scrap" and quarrel but you must not

[63]

shed blood: killing is taboo. It sets going that cancer of society, the blood feud. You may make your own pile as big as you like but you must not pilfer from anyone else's. The sex problem is hardly visible: it is taken for granted that there is no sex starvation. So you are not, on pain of death, to steal another man's wife. As to the fourth question, "What is a Promise?" or, its converse, "Does lying really matter?" the Decalogue again is pedestrianly practical. You may lie if you like as long as you do not lie in a court of law.

It will be seen that the Decalogue is not a preventive code. For, though it is law, it fails to pursue law to that scientific pitch that discovers that prevention is better than cure, that no man is free at the moment of action, and that as man has sown he will inevitably reap. It took Hebraism perhaps fifteen hundred years before it learned that out of the abundance of the heart the mouth speaks, that the heart must be watched for out of it comes all action, and that to look on a woman with lust is already to have committed adultery. Only toward one act is there a psychological reaction. In the case of a single sin is there realization that it is a state of mind that establishes guilt and commits crime. "Thou shalt not covet," is the one motive-commandment and, as it is a sin in the mind, it may well be a later addition to the law. For how can a law which punishes acts vouched for by two witnesses establish covetousness? The Decalogue's one penalty is death; a reign of terror would be set up by any attempt to enforce the law, as expressed in the tenth commandment. It is also worth noting that the only offense of thought is an offense to do with property. This is the code of a people already thinking mainly of wealth and so aware of the danger of such an obsession. This fact is additionally interesting when

[64]

we see that, though the question, "What is rightful wealth?" is already being subtly discussed the final question of the Five Interrogations is not even noticed. To "What is Death?" the Decalogue only remarks obliquely that if father and mother are honored, the children will obtain longevity.

It should, however, be noted also when considering the tenth commandment that the question which it attempts to answer, "What is Thought?" is one which must inevitably lead to that deepest of all questions, "What is Death?" For the larger question which is latent in the specific question, "What is wrong in the mere desire for the goods of another?" is, "What is Thought? Can mere thought affect anything?" Sanskrit philosophy has always maintained that thought itself is a power, a direct action, and therefore we are liable for damage which we may cause by our failure to control its power and action. Conversely, we can do good by the direct action of good thought. It is this fact that is held to be the *raison d'être* of the prayer of contemplatives. If evil thought is not only the ground but the seed of evil action, then good thought is the earth bed and germ of good action. This conclusion raises the further question: If thought is a real and direct power, and not merely a forerunning shadow of action, then what is consciousness? Is the psyche merely the shadow or wraith of the physique, or is consciousness a thing, a state, a being in its own right, *sui generis?* Further, if consciousness is *sui generis*, associated with a body, but not merely a symptom of that body, why should the death of that body destroy it and how does that event affect it? We therefore must come upon the final question, "What is Death?" And should that question be replied to by the answer, "Death is not the end of consciousness," then a new range of moral-

[65]

ity is revealed. Apparent failure and apparent success are neither of them necessarily the truth about life. The Jewish Decalogue's assumption that God must and does justify the righteous in this life may well be a complete misapprehension of the Divine Justice, a misapprehension as complete as to think that vitamin deficiency or vitamin intake must show their results in a day or a week. Once such creative doubts begin to stir in men's minds, a further revolutionary expansion is about to take place in the current concepts and definitions of natural moral law.

IV

The Law, Debt and Redemption

THE Decalogue marks, therefore, the type of answer given to the questioning challenge of law by post-Heroic man: man newly come to a sense of his individuality, an individualism verging on egotism already, but sufficiently aware of its problems to realize that it must find a balance between individual claims and social requirements. The Decalogue is then a balance rather than an integration. It is an adjustment of conflicting demands rather than a symbiosis. Its end is justice, mechanical justice, and so, in two regards it is unable to meet the actual demands of life. In the first place, it is not only non-preventive, it is not remedial. Its only process is amputation: "The soul that sinneth shall die." There is no redemption. It is clear that if a society is so loosely linked that it is only composed of individuals each watching to see that his neighbor shall not do what he would do if he dared, that society has no power nor wish to salvage one who fails. Secondly (and this is, in fact, a graver problem), such a code of crude justice, though it can roughly sanction a society whose physical inventions are as crude as its psychological insights, cannot prevent those inventions continuing. It is this fact that leads to the gravest consequences: for once more it disbalances the two sides of man's nature, the two aspects of his knowledge which must be equal to each other if he and his society are to

[67]

endure. We must never forget that there is a constant balance that must be maintained between cohesion and expansion, between conviction and speculation, between psychology, the knowledge of our own nature and physics, the knowledge of outer nature.

The Decalogue could not really balance man's nature, for not being a full definition of what he is, it could not give him understanding of himself and such satisfaction in his action as could content him. It tried to arrest, not to solve his emergent egotism. Hence his interest in the world of the senses, his absorption with that egotistic aspect of his consciousness which can only apprehend the material universe, became exclusive. He did not try to understand his own nature and "that beyond which is within," to which his deeper nature is a bridge. Hence inventions in the physical world came fast and furiously but the inner world was still perfunctorily summarized under legalistic anthropomorphism. Such a conception of the moral aspect of the universe prevented man from seeing that the moral law was so compelling, so self-sanctioning because it was part of all Law, and as natural, as helpful if kept, as fatal if flouted, as any law of physics. The egotist, whether he keep the moral law or break it, is always fatally ignorant, because he is blind to that wholeness of his nature of which the moral law is the scientific description.

A rigid canon and finally verbal inspiration were therefore imposed: an authority blind and inapposite, a letter that simply killed, because life could not grow in its rigid definition. The worst were determined to undermine it: the best were resolved to rise above it: only the timid and unthinkingly conventional supported it.

The inventions made in the outer world did, therefore,

gravely endanger man's estate, instead of benefiting it. Of these nothing was more important and significant than the invention of money. In the form of a widely circulating currency, money probably first appeared in Lydia in the eighth century and its effects were more socially disintegrating than even those which the discovery of iron weapons had provoked some three centuries earlier. A gold currency can be more destructive than an iron armory. The "Iron-bearing Lords," of Hesiod's wail, bore not more disastrously on the agriculturist than did the new money-lords whose plutocracy is so bitterly denounced by Amos. Indeed the very extravagance of their oppression drove men to a new effort to think morally and to develop psychological insight which might master this new fatally destructive convenience. It is a thought not without encouragement for our own capsized generation that man's moral inventions seem to spring as reactions from disasters caused by unbalanced physical and economic advances.

Certainly what we may call the second stage in the discovery and definition of moral law arose immediately after, and very largely because of, those economic discoveries, the most spectacular and disturbing of which was money. This was quite natural because the discovery of money is itself quite as much a psychological as an economic insight. The invoice, the check, the coin of currency are all both an advance in power of abstraction and also of "timebinding." If civilization is "the power to postpone satisfaction," then money is an essential implement to such a culture. Till then man's possessedness and possessiveness are confined to his power of storage, storage of perishables, as all really physical wealth must always be. The "Rich Fool" of the Gospels can only "pull down his barns and build greater": he cannot invest in unredeemable stocks.

[69]

The avaricious of the first century can be shown to be fools because rust will destroy the weapons and the locks with which they would insulate and preserve their wealth, while clothes moths and weevils will devour their apparel and food stores. Money makes wealth increasingly a social subjective idea, not an economic objective fact. Credit, and indeed any coin, is not a wealth I can be sure I have, as is a loaf of bread in the wilderness; it is only what other people may choose, or not choose, to go on thinking about certain social tokens which I am temporarily holding.

These facts are clearer to us who have lived through inflations and deflations, through going onto gold and going off, through free and controlled currencies, than they were to our grandparents. Hence credit, which money introduces, makes men think of wealth as a psychosocial thing. This has had three results, two of which make this crisis more acute and the third which helps toward solving it. The first we have seen: Money, the other name of which describes its essential use, currency, refuses to circulate. Man has a new *social* power and convenience in money but he still intends to use it as though he were simply an economic physiologically self-sufficient individual. Hence the capitalist and banker ruin the actual producer and especially the essential producer of the truest and therefore the most perishable wealth, the producer of food. Secondly, not only does there arise a plutocracy, which, practicing usury, bankrupts society. Money, because it is really more a psychological than an economic invention, though its psychosocial aspect is unrecognized, has increasingly morbid effects on men. The rich, when property is consumable goods, are people of display. They give a good show. Wealth is a synonym for plenty, for health, for a sort of friendliness of a fashion. (Compare the phrase in Daniel, "Fat and well-liking," and the Shakespearean Caesar's demand for those about him to be "fat and those who sleep o'nights.") But money-wealth is none of these, and the man who holds money most closely, who is always gaining and never giving, is called not fortunate but by the word of which the Latin meaning is wretched: a miser. Indeed an element of miserliness, a tendency to oversave, begins to mark all society and an oversaving society strangles itself in debt. That is of course what happened. Then there appear the classic reformers of this age, such as Solon of Athens; the first thing they must do is to ruin the savers to save the debtors whom the savers have ruined. The mass of people, the mainstay of production, are enslaved, bankrupt to the owners who themselves produce nothing and who cannot get their money back. For even if society would so prosecute itself to honor a mistaken word, not enough money exists to pay the debts and, if they were paid, the money would not turn into goods. Thus reformers of the Solon type sacrifice the unproducing minority, cancel all debts, create jubilee years when every promise to pay becomes void by a statute of limitations. They do not solve the problem, for they neither get rid of money nor try further to understand it. They fight its extension of usefulness when it develops interest and, finally, the culminating social genius, Aristotle, definitely decides money cannot be banished but that interest must never be permitted. This is a regression really to the individualistic socio-psychology of the Decalogue for it draws an arbitrary line between a thing, money, and its inevitable psychological consequences, credit, capital and interest.

This important development we shall be considering when we reach the Christian contribution to the Perennial Philosophy. So here all we need say further is that the moral solution to a new economic problem, caused by a physical discovery, is never to try to arrest the economic inventiveness but rather to advance psychological discoveries to the same level. This is obvious when we realize that the economic or physical inventions arise because man's mind is growing. Inventions are the symptoms and fruits of a consciousness evolving in definiteness. Whenever they become exclusively or predominantly economic and physical, that is because man's consciousness has not only become two-sided but because that one side which only sees the physical world is alone advancing. The division of man's mind may be inevitable in his evolution. What is disastrous is that his psychological insight should be arrested and make no discoveries. If such discoveries are made then man does advance in power, and he does preserve into a higher degree of awareness his happiness.

The third result of the economic revolution or mutation which produced money, was a psychological insight, a step toward remedying the economic chaos. As said above, money itself was a psychosocial discovery, though men did not realize it was, thinking it purely economic. The myth of Midas, the king in whose country money was probably first fully developed, shows that the Greek mind at least, suspected the catch that was hidden in currency. Dionysus gives the king power to turn everything he touches into gold; and the king starves. A deeper insight came from seeing that money is a social thing, a thing which has no worth—on the contrary is a profound social danger—unless it circulates, unless it is currency and unless it gives rise to credit, the power to give men freedom from immediate want that they may create more plenty, more power and more values in living.

Such an insight discovered, as we have seen, that avarice

and miserliness are, in the end, more socially dangerous than any actual pilfering. Even at Decalogue level the moral law, at least in one of its commandments, has shown that even men's thoughts, if they are evil, will bring misery to them as individuals and ruin to their society. The moral law is natural law able to sanction itself even in the secret places of the heart.

We can date these moral discoveries and advances as we can date the economic inventions that provoked them. What is called the Age of Conscience is, I want to repeat, not the dawn of conscience. That is at Decalogue level. The eighth to the seventh century B.C. is rather the high noon of the concept of man's individual responsibility, of the conviction that each soul is wholly and only liable for its own guilt and able to achieve its own salvation.

The Perennial Philosophy had, we have seen, managed to find some expression, strangulated but not quite inadequate, in that individualism, which, coming after the Heroic Age, began to realize the conception of law, both natural and moral. Four of the Five Questions have been answered in terms of acts to be forbidden. One of them, property, is already considered as needing a psychological inhibition as well. The fifth question, "What is Death?" is ignored or still latent. The whole of this Law, these answers show, is, as we should expect, individualistic and legalistic. That means that the Decalogue, taking individuals to be irreducible and inexpandable, constant unchanging units of consciousness, attempts justice, mechanic justice. It assumes, both that all men are responsible and are able to act as their individual bodily needs demand, and also that all men are separate. Each individual must and can pay his own debts and society is just and wise so to treat individuals, exacting the uttermost farthing, the eye, the tooth, the limb, and the very life if it is due. This, of course, is psychologically and anthropologically untrue. No man is self-made: he is part of his social heredity, how vastly so, studies of feral children have shown.[1] No man falls but the group is dragged down to some degree: no man is cut off but an invisible spiritual hemorrhage drains man's social vitality.

As, then, man's knowledge of himself grows in detail, and he wishes to bring that knowledge under his conception of law, he discovers two things: First, he sees that he must trace back events. Law means the recognition of causality. Hence he sees that each of the Five Questions points back before the actual event to the source of the event, that frame of mind which inevitably resulted in that specific act. In other words, he is no longer satisfied to be concerned with physical deeds but inquires into psychological states. The second discovery is not less important. He discerns that, though in many cases only one man commits the act, in perhaps as many cases the motive to that act may come from many individuals. The group therefore can not escape all liability for its individual who failed. To put the issue with legal brevity, man has then moved from the Law of Justice to the Law of Equity. The mechanic conception of Justice is being replaced by the organic conception of Equity. Should not, then, this discovery of a law of social, co-operative, organic living, instead of the enforced truce of competing individuals, have rebalanced the ship of man's evolution? Could he not now go forward, his physical and economic inventions balanced by his social and psychological insight? Would not his society now be sanctioned by an increasing knowledge of his actual nature, by his perception that, though apparently an individual,

[1] See Robert M. Zingg, *Wolf Child and Feral Man*.

[74]

he is in fact tied under the threshold of his individualized consciousness in a living circulation with his fellows, all "parts of a single continent"?

As we shall see, men did later go forward, and, in terms of the Law of Equity, give answers to all the Five Interrogations. But the first reaction to the discovery that law means the recognition of causality was hardly social at all; it was almost a secession from society.

We will take as our example the case best known. It is, we must remember, only a particularly well-known and consistent example. The Jains, who date from the same epoch, are even more consistent. Wherever men made this discovery of psychological causality they acted in this way. In Pali Buddhism we have men of what we may call the second prophetic generation, taking up monastic life. Psychological causality, or, to use its Sanskirt name, karma, made men aware that acts of the will had caused their present situation. As the Dhammapada says, "All that we are is due to what we have thought." But who is the thinker? Obviously not one's surface self. By thinking I cannot add one inch to my stature. But by that deeper affirmational thought called meditation, I can affect and alter, not merely my character and change my nature, I can alter bodily functions and even modify bodily organs. This is clear proof that there lies in me a power not my surface self, but which is much more powerful and has formed me. It was this discovery that made men, still so predominantly individualistic, conceive of the responsibility and the power which had made them what they were, as a power of physical heredity, as a narrowly linear Law of cause and effect. This inadequate notion had naturally three serious consequences. First, it gave rise to "Holy Selfishness," which is St. Jerome's approving phrase, for the doctrine of private

[75]

salvation. Secondly, it made heredity a material thing. My only problem was my own line of past incarnations. Hence my chief concern came to be liberation from the body: the flesh comes to be considered evil instead of menial. Thirdly, it disregards true human heredity, social heredity, and so fails to understand that life is a company of unlimited liability. The discovery occasions a double mistake —man deserts society and yet fails to liberate himself.

As took place with the discovery of money and the Law of Exchange, so with the discovery of heredity and the Law of Descent, a psychosocial law is narrowed by men, still only able to think of themselves as physical individuals, bound to a physical process.

But as with money men were forced, by the ruin caused through misconceiving its nature, to remedy their relationships towards a common responsibility, so with the discovery of the Law of Heredity. The mistake of thinking it a physical fact, an individual line of descent, caused a remedial reaction. Indeed, even Pali Buddhism of the Hinayana School found itself compelled by those valid empowering reasons of the heart, to live beyond its narrow definitions. Professor Hocking has called Karuna, the Compassion which is as cardinal in Hinayana as it is in Mahayana or Christianity, the "Noble Inconsistency." Yes, intellectually: No, psychologically. For the spirit of the individualized man seeking liberation from that private self which walls him up in a selfish body, cannot but see that the way to loose that suffocating strangle hold is by acts of love toward other prisoners. Buddhism immediately formed an order in which individuals could give one another essential help toward liberation. The Dhammapada says, "There is no deliverance for any outside the Sanga." Allow that, and you rule that private salvation is not possible. And Pali Buddhism lived up to its practical and cordial discovery. In the Order one not only finds salvation: one finds the urge for liberation of itself carrying one out to preach to all salvation from the self. There is no inconsistency here but rather a profound consistency that transcends the intellectualist mistake made by a still egoized consciousness, a mistake seen through directly the ego-distortion begins to be reduced. Indeed, Buddhism, far from being charged with an unmoral spiritual selfishness, may rather, in its actual practice, be accused of an undue spiritual generosity and prodigality.

Buddhism overlooked that advice given lasting form by Jesus: "Cast not your pearls before swine lest they turn again and rend you." Hinayana teaching can certainly sound the note of spiritual selfishness and secession from society, though here we must remind ourself that this note has also sounded through some of the most resonant of Christian teaching. I wonder whether in any Pali text can be found such defiant denial of any social responsibility as Tertullian's well-known defense of the Church's deliberate secession from mankind? "I am my own end. I care for nothing but to have no care. One can find a much better life in solitude than in society. Do you blame me as lazy and say one must live for one's city, for the empire, for society! These views prevailed formerly. But no one was born for others seeing that everyone has to die for himself."

Hinayana practice, certainly, was unlimited in its desire to give to everyone, regardless of his readiness, the wonderful find it had made. Buddhism, with a quixotic gallantry, a determination to help without delay, disregarding the very knowledge of the Law of Heredity which was the basis of its new insight and gospel of salvation, taught the highest liberation to all and sundry, denying caste. This is the

[77]

mistake of unthinking good will, certainly not one of a cold indifference. It was the disregard of that advice which has found modern expression through the most influential Humanist voice of today. It is Bernard Shaw, the grand-godfather of socialism, who has said, "The Golden Rule has two clauses, the first is, 'Do unto others as you would be done by,' and the second is, 'Don't!'" Modern scholarship, therefore, now recognizes Mahayana Buddhism to be an extension of Law, not a corruption. For the study of natural moral law showed that, as there was a linear psychophysical heredity, so there was also a convergent social heredity; as there is an individual karma so, as undeniably, there is a social karma.

With this discovery we are entering the field wherein vicarious suffering, atonement, redemption all now become matters of actual knowledge, of actual observation of the life process. This is not the abolition of Law; it is its enlargement until in the Law of Love, the Law is completely fulfilled by the total redemption of the whole. This again is a vast subject most easily studied in the specific Christian emphasis.

Here we have still to consider in its five specific details, the second answer to the Five Questions—the answer of justice, that is, the individualistic mechanic justice illustrated by the Decalogue and the answer of Equity. The specific answers of Equity to the Five Interrogations are well worth attention. They are also very hard to detect. For, as a historic fact, though Equity is again and again seen to be necessary, though it is again and again demonstrated that the legal letter kills, men fail to discover the Law of Equity, and when they do discover it, fail, by misnaming it, to recognize what they have found. The great prophet of the Exile, Ezekiel, as the Hinayana texts of

Buddhism, stated over and again absolute individual responsibility. This, however, prevents a complete social reply to the Five Questions. A doctrine of private salvation always spells social arrest. Indeed all the speakers of the prophetic age are passionate individualists and therefore pre-anthropological. "You shall not say, 'The Fathers have eaten sour grapes, and the children's teeth are set on edge,' " cries Ezekiel with a gallant wish to assert free will. But the proverb-maker was nearer the truth than the prophet. The solution of the problem of free will is to be found not in narrowing human responsibility, but in enlarging it; in accepting what justice calls another's fault through love's power of seeing that other, though alienated by his sin, as still oneself.

Hence neither the prophets, nor the new lawgivers (Ezra, Buddha, Zoroaster), nor the social reformers, such as Solon, work out fully the second answer to the Five Interrogations, the Equity answer. Their individualism blinds them to the psychological sanction for socialism, i.e., that man is always more than an ego. They do, therefore, one of two things. If they are socially concerned, their individualism makes them believe that the problem of new powers can be solved, and society be salvaged, by just getting rid of those recent inventions. They are so individualized themselves that they cannot see that these new inventions are resultant symptoms of individualism. They fail to push back their tracking of causality far enough to recognize that a split psyche will result in an egotistic foreconsciousness. They do not see that such a partial consciousness, absorbed with the world of the senses, will multiply power inventions there, regardless of the consequences such inventions will have upon purpose and meaning: and that the sunken and submerged part of consciousness which once manifestly united

[79]

each with his fellows, will neither bridge the chasm nor will it be able to make spiritual discoveries contemporarily equal with the physical discoveries being made by the ego.

Hence, as we have seen, the Solons of Greece and their counterparts in the Hebrew world cancel all debts and proclaim jubilee years. Their successors, such as Aristotle, condemn outright all interest. Lycurgus in Sparta shows the symptom-obsessed mind of the individualist even more pathetically. He will permit iron money only. As a result, nearly every Spartan general was bought up when he went abroad, with gold! At this period the one reform of all these reformers is worse than trying to put back the clock. For not only do they try to avoid the consequences of the invention while still retaining the invention itself (money); they completely fail to recognize the source and cause of unbalanced physical invention—the mutation in, and fracture of, the primal unified consciousness. Hence their one program is to get men back to what they imagine original society to have been (compare Hosea's "I will allure thee back into the wilderness"). A similar attempt was made during the 1918-1939 Armistice to get rid of war by reducing arms and forbidding the use of new war inventions. But such an imagination is completely unhistorical. This misconception is the reverse of the genie and the bottle. There the problem was to reduce and recondense a vast pervasive spirit back into a flash. The insoluble problem which the social reformers of the seventh and eighth centuries were attempting was how to make consciousness, which had condensed into the hard granules of egotistic individualism, re-expand into the homogeneous atmosphere of social integration. They could not even state their problem in psycho-anthropological terms. Their method was individualistic justice: their goal a society of individuals made

[80]

just by being forbidden to employ certain resultants of individualistic methods: their arguments, that man must and can keep the Law of Justice because every man is equal and is an equally responsible individual (and must be killed if he does not), were demonstrably false.

The other course is taken by those prophet reformers whose individualism makes them so suspicious of the state that they seek only to save individuals, maintaining that society exists only for individuals and *is* nothing but a number of individuals. They therefore seek and teach liberation from all the ties of society and family; and they teach this liberation is possible and necessary for all, here and now in this life. To the Five Interrogations they would give only the most radical answer. They do not attempt the middle stage of Equity, the stage of the Higher Law, but urge all to adopt the Highest Law, the Law of Love, of universal compassion, of giving without return, of unlimited service without any wage. To those incapable of making such a sacrifice, to those tied by wife and children, they have nothing clear to offer, no middle way. Hence the only course open to the ordinary man of good will is to fall back on the Law of Justice. Again we must leave this development until we can watch it fully grown in Christianity.

What we can see is that for the time being, the moral effort and progress of man as a social being was arrested. Man's spiritual progress was divided between two efforts, both of which had entered a blind alley. On the one hand were the social reformers whose only solution is an archaistic society, a society of individuals arbitrarily forbidden to use certain economic inventions made by the individualistic mind (and therefore bound to be reinvented) and not taught how to make balancing psycho-

[81]

logical inventions. On the other are the founders of monastic orders whose only solution is to end mankind in that generation. How man's social development was again brought forward and how the celibate contributed to that (by being the father of the social heredity) we shall see later.

It is, however, worth noting here that the Five Basic Moral Requirements made by Buddhism of both sorts on religious and laity alike are five answers to the Five Questions. They are: Not to Kill, Not to Steal, Not to Lie, Not to commit Adultery, and the fifth, in answer to "What is Thought?" is the rule, Never to take Intoxicants. This, obviously, is to guard against the chief danger of any loss of responsibility or full awareness.

V

The Law of Justice Superseded by the Law of Equity

YET as an actual fact, both in the reformed societies and in the monastic orders, progress in detecting the extent and processes of moral law did continue.

It will, therefore, help us to recognize such advances if we make clear in specific detail what are the actual answers to the Five Interrogations given by the Higher Law, the Law of Equity. This Law of Equity we may call the Law of Co-operation or the Law of Life, to distinguish it from the mechanic Law of Justice and the spiritual Law of Love. It must, as we have said, be a construction, for, as a code, the Law of Equity was never promulgated and indeed we shall have to reach the second age of Christianity before we shall find it working as a fairly complete, though unrecognized, system.

We have seen that the Decalogue (and the codes or conventions of the same spiritual horizon) gives as its answers to the Five Interrogations, four practical inhibitions: practical for two reasons, because they deal with actions, not thoughts, and because they can be obeyed. This second practicality, we must repeat, is of great importance. For we are so used (being brought up in Paulinism) to conceive of moral law as something that cannot be fulfilled and which therefore is an accuser, an enemy, an executioner. Law which cannot be kept is of course deadly. Law which can be kept is a way of life, deliverance, creativity. "This do and thou shalt *live*," is the rightful claim of Law, and man's response is, "Thy Law is a light on my path, a lamp to my footsteps." The four practical inhibitions which can be observed are: Not to kill, to steal, to take another's wife, to swear falsely.

Equity arises when the Five Interrogations are faced by men who understand by studying natural moral law that individualistic mechanic justice does not meet the actual facts; does not answer exactly enough the questions, What are Force, Property, Sex, a man's Word and Death? Equity's answer will, therefore, be to follow up and trace back the four vetoes of justice to their psychological sources, to the springs of action. The normal man can normally keep the factual Law, the Law of Deeds. But in abnormal circumstances and under abnormal pressures, he may fail; if, for example, he is robbed of his land by a usurer, he may, when starving, steal. A man with an abnormally weak head may be persuaded by friends with stronger heads to become fighting drunk and commit manslaughter. True justice, therefore, must trace the real blame not only to the doer but to the provocatants. True justice must not only trace the sources but having found them must staunch them. It must aim at censuring and preventing certain states of mind found to be predisposing to criminal acts.

So this tracing back leads to a profounder discovery. We discover we are not the individuals we thought we were. Justice says, "Here is the guilty: here is the guiltless sufferer. See: the man who struck is proved to be the criminal for he did the deed." "No," says Equity, "the other may have provoked him." "That's hairsplitting!" says the Decalogue. But Equity wins, for it is in fact true. Beside the

[84]

murderer there can be the murderee, and bloodshed may then not be murder but "justifiable homicide."

Hence the Law of Equity is two new things: It is psychological in a double sense: first, in that it recognizes motive as being more significant than action, and secondly, and even more importantly, because it recognizes to some degree joint responsibility. "It takes two to make a quarrel" is a typical finding of Equity and gradually this significant ruling is extended to the four directly social Interrogations. It takes two to commit adultery. Criminal negligence is a contributing factor to theft; and credulity, too often a wish to be deceived, creates the climate of deceit in which the loosest tongue utters the lie other ears wish to hear.

Nor is Equity, in tracing back responsibility, able to stop with two, the doer and the done-to, the aggressor and the sufferer. It has to begin to see that the whole community must accept some responsibility for all individuals within it and for all their acts. The Decalogue is negative. It tells what must not be done, and the one reward it offers is longevity. It leaves the individual to find the worth of life in himself, indeed to find that worth so amply that still, under all the restrictions it imposes, he will find life worth while. The attitude of the Decalogue to human psychology is analogous to that of many of the trade-unions to the capitalists. They take no responsibility for profit making; they say *that* is the employer's concern. All they insist is that, regardless of the problems of sales and production costs, the employer must pay the wages the union standard of life demands. The Law of Equity is radically different in this respect and more anthropological. It is positive both in its demands and in its rewards. For the power to fulfill the Law, and the rewards given by the Law, lie in the community at least as much as in the individual. The com-

[85]

munity is the individual's inspirer, his helper when he fails, and in its life and approbation consists his reward.

We see this when we realize that when the conception of the Higher Law enters man's mind he is able to recognize that cutting off the criminal has proved to be a mistake. Death or imprisonment—neither is a solution. The individual must be restored. The group must acknowledge some degree of joint error in the actual analysis of causes, if society is not to be injured by the loss or alienation of a member. This discovery leads to still another. If acts spring from thoughts and thoughts from the standards practiced by a community, then we must and can trace back the source of error. That no man is free at the moment of action, is the negative warning pointing to a solution: The more prevention the less need of cure. The sooner an aberration is recognized, the easier it is to correct. Foresight is the kindness of kings, for he who has the farthest vision, the clearest detection of causality, has the greatest power over events, and needs to use less force to guide them. Freedom is increasingly won by him who can force back further and further his recognition of beginnings. Always it is true, "The first step I am master not to take." And to know how far back that first step lies is the whole task and process of enlightenment.

Now what are the answers of Equity to the Five Interrogations? To the first question, "What is Force?" Equity answers, "To object to bloodshed is both too little and too much. Anger is the source of murder. Anger, too, being vindictive leads to revenge. It treats the object as something to be destroyed. This is a mistake. You must ban and bar the wrong deed, and the doer only so long as he persists in the deed."

Such principles are easy to applaud but hard to apply.

[86]

The Decalogue works well enough as long as men's natural instruments, physical powers and economic contracts are simple, fairly weak and limited to a single group. But when material inventions increase, owing to the increasing intensity of the sense-world absorbed ego-consciousness, men can increase envy and avarice by amassing goods and deal increasing damage. They will also meet many people outside their own social group and not under the same code of conduct. Equity is necessary to balance invention. But when we come to the question, "What is Force?" Equity's answer is mixed. It denies that force is unlimited violence and cunning. It would allow that the force of argument is the real force, that a clear moral case can go far to adjust a dispute. Equity has then, I believe, two answers to the force question, what may be called the internal and the external answer. The internal answer is comparatively simple: it is Arbitration, the use of a legal umpire or referee to settle legal disputes between men of the same law, under the same jurisdiction. This is a natural development, because such a community has come to realize to a considerable degree its common responsibility. The wish to use the law as a weapon against one's neighbor appears increasingly as undesirable as it is useless. The end of law is to adjust two claims, each of which has some right, neither a total justification.

The external answer is far more difficult. For what can Equity rule when someone who does not acknowledge our code attacks us and uses unlimited violence and cunning? Three replies are possible: (1) to combine all those who share the code of Equity and so by superior numbers but limited violence to withstand the aggressor; (2) to forestall the attack by yielding to every reasonable demand that the aggressor may make: (3) to practice nonviolence. The first reply has been tried and failed. The second has never been attempted with the thoroughness and persistence which would allow us to know whether it could succeed.[1] The third reply would not be the answer of the Higher Law of Equity but of the Highest Law of Love. We must then postpone that consideration till we reach that development.

What did, historically, take place was the rise of chivalry. The theory of chivalry is that physical force is necessary to keep order among states. An army must, then, be employed. But it must fight by strict rules; only certain weapons may be employed; ambushes and all trickery are disallowed; indeed, if the other side lacks a certain arm, such as a corps of elephants, the side that has the temporary advantage must wait. Those who yield or fall must be spared. The conclusion of the Bhagavad-Gita gives the classic description of such chivalric warfare. And into the eighteenth century A.D. an attempt was being made thus to carry the principles of the duel into full-scale battle when the French were able to address their British enemies with the courteous invitation, "Let the gentlemen of the Guard fire first." It is necessary to grasp these principles of chivalry, though actual adoption of them may have been rare, because of the pivotal part chivalry has played in all ordered society and especially in the thought and organization of Christendom. I venture to suggest that chivalry does work at its actual level, meaning by its actual level that stage of the evolution of consciousness when two conditions are present. The first of these we have seen: It is that state of readjusted balance after the earlier balance between

[1] But as De Lict has shown in his work on this subject, history contains far more cases of the successful employment of this method than the ordinary reader or historian realizes.

physical knowledge and psychological knowledge had been upset by the ego's obsession with physics. This readjustment is achieved by advancing psychological knowledge as far as physical inventions have advanced. It is advanced psychological knowledge which makes possible such conceptions as the laws of nations, the rules of war, the discipline of military vows, which together give rise to the idea of chivalry. The power of that idea lies in the belief that there is a loyalty which extends beyond all frontiers and embraces all who share its training and obligations.

The attitude to war is that there are recurrent occasions of conflict, incidental outbreaks, like small epidemics in a community otherwise healthy enough. These outbursts pass because civilization's cohesion lies not in arms but in a common honor, not in force of weapons but in an embracing good sense. The armed knight is necessary, the mounted squad in the king's stable (the constables) to be ready to check the passionate hastiness with which a minority, swayed by an intemperate leader, may attempt to take the law into its own hands. When the law has spoken, when intemperance has been shown that it cannot succeed in such assaults on the common order, then tempers cool and peace returns. Restraint being used without vindictiveness, rancor does not ensue and revenge is therefore not bred. Here, in germ, is the notion of an international police force, a notion which, though it never actualized fully, remains haunting the social mind of man. A further factor that must be present fixing that level at which chivalry may emerge (let alone mature) is another state of balance. All the communities between whom chivalry functions, as the final adjuster and arbiter of force, must be at the same level of invention, i.e., their physical inventions must not utterly outrun their psychological discoveries.

[89]

It is here, I also venture to suggest, we discover the reason why chivalry, which worked in the past, is helpless today as a solution of the problem of force. For today this balance between physical invention and psychological discovery has been utterly upset. Our so-called civilization has made the most fatal of all mistakes. It is possible, as Chinese civilization often did, to shut out aliens, keeping one's culture and one's craft, one's insights as to social cohesion and one's powers over matter, secret, to oneself. The Chinese empire and the Japanese nation repeatedly attempted to adopt this attitude to outsiders. Aggression, we must confess, was persistently taught them by the West. It is possible, as Byzantine civilization long survived by doing, to have competitive contacts with powerful political neighbors but to keep as an essential secret the physical inventions, such as the various forms of Greek Fire and the formulae for the Damascene steel, which gave victory in battle. What is fatal is to deal with peoples whom we consider barbarian, never to be treated as equals and to be exploited, and yet in dealing with them to give these peoples access to our physical methods of material inventiveness. We must return to this supremely critical and topical issue when discussing, in the frame of Christendom, the Law of Equity and its answer to the question, "What is Force?"

Equity's answer to the second question, "What is Property?" also shows the realization that society and individual are both far more complex and interfused entities than was conceived by the individualism of the Decalogue. Property is not mine to do with as I like regardless of the others whose observance of my rights alone permits me to enjoy possession. Conversely, the community has an obligation, and not merely a right, toward me. I am a member of a living body; member and body are bound to care for each other. We have seen that the reformers, such as Solon, who were called in to clear up the first financial smash caused by money, tried to put things back. "Back to normalcy with Solon" was no doubt his winning slogan. But there is no going back in life, no unthinking what has been thought and uninventing what has been invented. Invention can be driven underground, that is all. Small secessionist communities, finding that they no longer need practice an exacting invented skill, may give up the art or science, as birds left long on protected islands lose their wings.[2] It is not known, however, that any people who once discovered money ever abandoned its use.

Further, we know that there did go on some social invention which could hope to balance economic invention and which would permit such devices as capital and interest to be used with safety. We know that Hillel in the first Century B.C. was concerned with modifications of the Law of Jubilee to make its swing against usury less unjust to the lender. The complex problems of bankruptcy are at least beginning to be recognized. The development of this particular invention, Bankruptcy Law, is slow but with its emergence we may say that we are getting the "negative" aspect of Equity's answer to "What is Property?" Bankruptcy Law says in effect: The social solution of debtor and lender is not a simple and purely economic matter of free individuals whose claims and counterclaims can be settled by mechanical justice. Nor can the matter be settled by just letting the debtor go scott-free. There must be an "adjustment," both debtor and creditor giving something, and, what is more, and most important, the community

[2] For example, the Maori's loss of the art of clinker-built boat construction. See Rivers, *The Decay of Useful Arts.*

[91]

standing behind them both as surety and as maker-up of the balance.

This is, however, "negative" because it is palliative, not preventive. The "positive" answer of Equity to the question, "What is Property?" was even slower at being uttered. The preventive invention which would guard against these exploitations which economic inventiveness causes or allows, is Co-operation. This device is, apparently, lacking throughout the ancient world. That Equity took so long a time to discover this, its specific answer to the economic question, "What is Property?" is probably to be explained by three considerations. In the first place, the village community was still throughout the ancient world the stable pattern of mankind, and in such simple agricultural communities there is the tradition which goes back to pre-individualistic collectivism. Secondly, neither the priest nor the knight, the *sacerdos* and the *rex,* is interested in production economics. One sanctions, the other defends; neither produces. Thirdly, the merchant, at first, is simply a broker, and for his type of mental skill the artist philosopher and the gentleman-athlete knight have a natural contempt, while the agriculturist has a not entirely unholy fear of it. The merchant, because of this his social heredity, is rated low in most social patterns. Call a man a huckster and he will be slow to become a hero or in any way magnanimous. One who has won for himself a begrudged position in society by sharp practice, by using law to extract the uttermost farthing, will find it difficult to discover co-operation, the economy of Equity, even when the society he lives in has turned the man at arms into the chivalrous knight, the man of honor. Indian society is mainly based on agriculture; so the Vaisya, the merchant, is only one step above the Sudra, the lowest caste. Chinese society, however, more dependent on trade and less dependent on the knight, demotes the soldier and promotes the merchant.

It was the third question, "What is Sex?" that led to most confusion in Equity's attempt to answer fully the entire Five Interrogations. Again we shall have to wait till we reach Christendom's working out or working toward Equity, before we can see this difficulty and lack of definition creating its gravest confusion. Here we may say that the question of sex is always a double one, not only man and woman, but also the personal psyche and the community. Further, it is agreed by all observers, that man often advances at woman's expense. The new state can hardly be said to mark moral progress but is rather an exchange of one injustice for another. With the end of the matriarchal phase and the rise of violence in the place of collective suggestion, woman tends to sink to the level of a chattel. The exchange was of the physical vice of something verging on male promiscuity, for a moral vice, jealousy and passionate possessiveness. The end of the matriarchal epoch is probably paralleled by the decline of the Life Religion into the Fertility Religion, the worship of motherhood and fecundity—Hera, queen of heaven, "the mothering air"—degenerating into the worship of eroticism and sex—Aphrodite. This would, and evidently did, lead to a period of promiscuity which the patriarchal heroic phase stamped out. The promiscuity at the close of the matriarchal Life Religion epoch, may have been the cause of its failing. Certainly without continence, spiritual prestige is impossible and, lacking spiritual prestige, woman is helpless before man, and a peaceful society impotent before a warrior state.

But, as we know, in spite of its vaunted puritanism, a patriarchal society may have strict laws about adultery while in actual fact there is a low standard of sexuality. A chivalrous society can have generous and even trustful standards toward a foe but sanction mean and cruelly suspicious behavior toward a wife (e.g., the Crusaders and the cinctures of chastity). "Progress in sexual hygiene depends on the improvement of woman's position," we say. But we must analyze that slogan. First, we must recognize that the emancipation of woman may actually lead, for the time being, to a relapse—or perhaps one should say, to a morbid aberration—in specifically sexual behavior. It certainly seems so today. What a man denied himself in order that he might have a faithful wife and might know that the children he raises are his own, he may find pointless, if woman wins the dubious right of indulgence. Promiscuity is dangerous, and (like most social aberrations really dangerous to man) is also rare. There is certainly no sign of promiscuity either in the so-called primitive cultures or among animals. Promiscuity is late, and, as Unwin has pointed out in *Sex and Culture*, has an ugly correlation with societies in a final state of dissolution. We may also say that promiscuity can be correlated with woman attaining the same analytically critical ego-consciousness as have men. Women have become men's equals in four fatal freedoms: Freedom from creative imagination, through obsession with the sensory world; freedom from conscience, through indifference to, and ignorance of, the unseen; freedom from awe, through unquestioning belief that everything can be understood and controlled by analysis; and freedom from inspiration through unawareness of the part which integral thought must take in any creative act.

So, secondly, when we examine the relations between woman's progress and a general improvement in sexual

[94]

behavior, we must note that woman's progress is the same as man's, not, in itself, either a moral improvement or a regression, but an opportunity and a demand that the Perennial Philosophy shall be restated in contemporary individualized terms. Woman is attaining to that detached consciousness which will give new powers, if its freedom from racial consciousness is not let end in the blind alley of self-consciousness, but can attach itself to a meaning greater than racial consciousness. We must note too that woman's consciousness divided later than did man's. Since woman is nearer to life, her detachment is delayed; anthropological evidence certainly sustains this. For example, among the Arunta (as Spencer and Gillen have observed) and in all such Stone Age Australoid cultures, women take no part in the religious feasts, because they do not have to restore in themselves the sense of union with Life. The threshold between conscious and paraconscious has not yet arisen. That original social descent is matrilinear and rulership matriarchal, is not because the woman is equal to man as a resourceful executive, but because, until the ligature in man's consciousness has completely separated him from his submerged consciousness, he knows that "hunch" is necessary and, as he feels he is losing it, he uses the woman's. The Deborah and Barak epic in the Book of Judges is one illustration of this.

It is not woman's lack of physical force that retards her in this matter of social position. Were that the criterion, the gorilla and not man would have ruled the primates. Man rules because he invents tools. Woman, emerging later into that ego-consciousness which is absorbed in managing the world of the senses, was behindhand. Man had the advantage of being the first to be at home among tools; compare a nineteenth century kitchen with a carpenter's shop. But, further, woman's symbiotic relationship with man demanded and demands imperatively that because he had become unbalanceably successful in analysis, she should deliberately retain her power of integral thought. Her "hunch" was necessary to keep the family ark from capsizing. Seership is essentially a woman's gift. Few things in religious history are more interesting than the tracing of the way in which the Delphic priesthood and the early Christian Church availed themselves of that easy pass over the range of the limen into the lost country of the paraconscious afforded by the woman's mind.

It may be said that in historic times the wizard is as common as the sibyl, and the prophet commoner than the prophetess. But this is related to the rise of celibacy and to the convergence of the sexes with the emergence of intergrades. This is a subject of great psychological interest, social importance and biological value but beyond the range of this present essay. We must repeat that only when man is completely sure that the answer to all his need in the physical world does he finally break with "hu. and despise the sibyl. Woman, after that, can only be courtesan, cook or comforter. Her deep desire for motherhood may spoil her for the first role: her deep wish to meditate may be as fatal to fulfilling the other two. If the contemplative life of the religious house be forbidden her, she has no choice but to go to college. The effect of that upon the birthrate we know. Woman's being educated pretty certainly plays a large part in the divorce rate, also. As Earl Russell, that much-concerned, much-experienced mathematician turned sociologist, has said, the difficulty of marriage is far more than doubled, and we may add its casualty rate rises catastrophically, when instead of one critical mind trying to put up with an uneducated partner there are two critical minds determined to settle every domestic difference by argument.

What, then, is the social solution offered by Equity when it would answer the question, "What is Sex?" We may say, though the phrase may not be easy to define and even more difficult to illustrate: Sacramental Marriage. Until marriage, which must not be unduly delayed, continence is expected. In the marriage itself, the obligation of partnership is put first, that obligation which is above all for others, of carrying on life by the incarnation of eternal spirits. In the relationship a bond of honor subsists between the parties which goes deeper and is more enduring than passion. It is a symbiosis; the aim is not the mistaken one of equality of two unfusable individuals, but of complementariness. Not only are the physiological duties, functions and interests different though intimately combined: this obtains with economic activities and with the things of the mind. A woman's intelligence, if she has the sense and independence to preserve her specific mental gift, is neither equal nor inferior to man's; it is complementary. Man can rationally analyze and criticize a proposition. Woman can give as valuable a reaction by that sudden insight we call hunch but which is perhaps better named integral thought. Sacramental Marriage, like all partnerships and trusts between responsible persons, looks very seriously upon its bond. Probably divorce is never considered as long as there are children to be affected by it; that would be a breach of the essential contract. As responsibility, respect and tenderness are its chief elements, the problem of sex—as today it has become both narrow and disproportioned, i.e., strangulated—is reduced again to a concern not to be disregarded but neither to be permitted to dictate to a truly whole and healthy person. The baby, I

[97]

understand, is today being taught that its needs will not be flouted but its whine for constant attention will be disregarded. If the baby can learn—and I am told he does— why despair of our adult selves?

There remains the last of the social interrogations: "What is your Word?" Equity has much to say on that. The Law of Justice confines one's word to one's oath, to one's sworn signature and to the letter of one's bond. Equity makes lying always a sin, the particular sin of the gift of speech. The social value of raising the spoken statement, and especially the promise, to the level of sanctity, is vast. Indeed it has important beneficial effects on all the other social questions: force, property and sex. Physical force can be greatly reduced if a man's word is his bond. A man of honor is not only a knight, he is a man who gives and cannot break his word of honor. The chivalric phase which preceded the rise of the Persian empire was marked by these men having three essential accomplishments and disciplines: "to ride the horse, shoot the bow, and speak the truth."[3] In societies where promises are respected, a misdemeanant can be excused imprisonment and fine and simply "bound over to keep the peace." The control, protection and extension of business are increased, if, like the early Quaker and the late Chinese merchant, the trader's word is his bond, and he observes the spirit of his agreements, renouncing the freedom to relieve himself of his promises when they have become disadvantageous to him. This standard is well set out in what is in consequence often called "the Gentleman's Psalm," Psalm 15, the key phrases of which are, "He hath not given his money out at usury nor sworn to deceive his neighbour. . . . He swears

[3] See Xenophon's *Cyropaedia*.

to his neighbour and disappoints him not, though it were to his own injury."

The word of honor has even more remarkable and beneficial effects in the conduct of sex. The promise, the "plighted troth," cannot be broken at the giver's convenience nor on his (or her) construction of the ruling that "circumstances alter cases." True, they do: but the maxim of law "that no man can be judge of his own case," forbids the person who is provoked to break the bond in order to release himself by his own judgment or when honor is highly rated, even by his own appeal.

Equity's power to raise so high the promise and the given word as guard against the lie, is undoubtedly correlated with Equity's answer to the final interrogation, "What is Death?" As the plighted word of honor vastly strengthens social security, in the use of force, in preservation of property and in guaranty of the home, so, in turn, the plighted word is powerfully buttressed by Equity's answer to the fifth question. Indeed we should remark here that the Five Interrogations are five pointer readings made on different aspects of a single law. The five rules are really the contours of a giant molecule.

The answer of the Law of Justice to the question, "What is Death?" is rudimentary. The Law promises that those who keep it shall have material prosperity, though it really cannot guarantee this. As to those who transgress, the Law can only maintain (and as inaccurately) that if it succeeds in cutting off the offending member he and his evil will cease. Equity, however, takes the first step in the understanding of death. It can do so, because in tracing causality, it began to find the roots of action and responsibility running out far beyond the individual and even beyond his generation. Descent, both in physical and social heredity, must be taken into account, if true responsibility is to be allotted. The past is a living past, living in us, who gain and lose by it. The full implications of this must be considered when dealing with the Christian theory of forgiveness. Here we can only say that as the tracing of responsibility, through the extensions of causality, leads man to see that the individual is a living part of a much greater whole, so, too, he begins to see that the individual need not be an arbitrary extrusion of consciousness out of a stream of unconscious biological succession. The God who is the God of the Patriarchs is not the God of the dead but of the living.

VI

The Rise of the Law of Love

WE HAVE now tried to reconstruct the answers of the Higher Law, the Law of Equity, to the Five Interrogations. It is a reconstruction, similar to those made by paleontologists from fossil remains. In this science the completed skeleton may not only be made out of bones coming from different sites but, here and there, a plaster model is fabricated to take the place of a particular intermediate bone not yet actually discovered but the shape and position of which can be deduced.

Up to this point we have made a construction of the model of the complete answer given by the Law of Equity to moral knowledge when that knowledge has discovered causality and responsibility to be greater than was perceived by the simple individualism of the Decalogue. The caste system in India may well be not earlier than the Aryan invasions, invasions by a culture the social heredity of which can be dated, in the evolution of consciousness, by the fact that it is late-Heroic, patrilinear and patriarchal, chivalrous and sun-worshiping. Such a culture is, we have seen, very far from primitive. Its primal integral consciousness has long divided into a foreconsciousness concerned with analytic sensory action and a subconscious concerned with integral thought. The protoindividual priest—king of the late Fertility rites—is therefore now divided into the Brahmin and the Kshatriya, the *sacerdos* and the *rex*. We may add, then, that, as the tracing of moral causality has begun to transcend the bounds of the individual life and the surface will, so the realization of the Nature of Things, the Essence behind the appearances, has begun to transcend that first attempt at Transcendence, that picture of a Sun Father God which makes Him the patriarchal Lawgiver, who by His Power sanctions a moral code otherwise sanctionless. The Transcendent Immanence of God begins when a deeper insight into Law discloses that the Law is not in two separate sections, one the sanctioning cosmology and the other the resultant ethic, but the two are interactant. Not only is natural moral law as self-sanctioning as is natural physical law, but moral law because it is natural law throws intellectual Light on natural physical law. Knowledge is a function of being, and the moral law, which is an essential method of our growth in consciousness, must therefore contribute to fresh knowledge of the body, society and the environment. Conversely, progress in knowledge of the environment sheds light on moral nature, and shows each individual that he is much more than an individual, and that he must realize his full nature. The conception of God becomes not merely that of a Lawgiver and Enforcer, nor that of a Law, but of an educator who educates by giving his creature Lawful Freedom.

This conception of the Fatherhood of God, I would then suggest, is post-Decalogue: it is the specific theology of the Law of Equity. It represents that stage of theology in which the *Philosophia Perennis* expresses itself when consciousness can detect Law as transcending the mechanical justice of individualism. It is, as ever, a knife-edge: for, always, the Eternal Gospel shines a fine belt of life-giving radiation between two extremes that go out into darkness. Here the extremes are, on the one hand, that wish to have an arbitrary God who because He is a being capable of emotional moods "will not always be chiding" and can be made relent if mollified and "met half way"; on the other hand, in reactions to such caprices, the idea of Law so inflexible that in the end any idea of a Lawgiver disappears behind a blind incomprehensible Necessity. As we shall see, Calvin is the midwife who presents the world with the devouring monster called mechanism. If, as Aurobindo Ghose in *Studies in the Gita* remarks, "God is not imprisoned in His own Transcendence," we may add neither is He codified in His own Law. Law and Grace are compatible because, as we have seen, Law is that high statistical probability, that Law of High Numbers, which permits us to know that we are in a rational universe. While Grace is that freedom of Low Numbers, which shows the individual that he is free to act by his experience of Lawfulness, that he may learn by his mistakes and that "the nature of things" does receive back the repentant and permit a new start.

In some such slight outline we may then detect the profile of the social pattern, the moral code and the theology given by the Higher Law, the Law of Equity, as it interprets and answers the Five Interrogations. But human society did more when it attained defined specificity of function, as it did in the caste system of the Laws of Manu with the priest and the king, the merchant and the servant. It not only became specialized in itself, it began to throw off special forms. From the idea of a priest, who was not the directive mind nor the hand nor the foot of the body politic but its eye, there emerged a further detachment, the monk. In Chapter IV this extreme specialization was referred to. It was shown that progress in Equity was confused and even arrested because the highest types tended to forsake the family and, relieved of that problem, to apply themselves, not to the answer of the Higher Law, the answer of Equity, but to the answer of the Highest Law, the Law of Love. The origins of celibacy cannot lie very deep in the historic record, yet they are difficult to trace. The Shaman type of witch doctor or dervish prophet may go back to the dawn of individualism. At that horizon there was probably a division. When the threshold appeared between the foreconscious and the subconscious, dividing the primal consciousness, the majority threw in their lot with the foreconscious and let the rest of their power and apprehension slide and sink into what was henceforward to be the subconscious. But a few choose the other way. They elected to follow that aspect of their awareness that was more interested in thought than in sensation, in integral apprehension than in critical analysis, in the world of ideas than that of senses, in the beyond that is within than in the so-called outer world of matter. The reason why they survived may well be because of their importance to societies that, without such experts, had to depend only and wholly for understanding on the use of the five senses. We must remember that man is the only creature to whom it ever occurs even to try such a onesided exploration. All animals, many possessing finer, and even additional, senses than man's, at every crisis of their lives—mating, rearing young, migrating —all turn to and rely on an inherent insight which is extrasensory.

And as we shall see, man, even when open vision is lost and inspiration is dead, still hardly ever is so rash as to trust solely his senses. He will still retain a moral tradition, a series of inhibitions which, though they cannot help him to create, will, at least, guard him against collapse into anarchy. He will then be aware of the social use of the type which retained awareness of the integral extrasensory consciousness. The value that society attached to such types is seen by their usual names: seer, prophet, wizard. He is the one who has an insight, a vision into, not only the meaning of events but the fog of time. He is wise, with a wisdom superior to the shrewdness of the practical "canny" man, who can act now, but who cannot say what will happen. His other side is shown by his other name: the wizard is uncanny; he is necessary, maybe, but never nice. Second sights acts generally as a warning, not an encouragement. His other name is madman, a fool. The royal jester, the one man licensed to tell the despot the truth and treat his power simply as appearance, is the vestigial remnant of the court seer. The dervish is the madman who has to be mad to this world if he is to be a sane seer of that other world wherein the wisdom and canniness of this world is foolishness. The later form of the seer, the bard, must figuratively be blind, indeed he is sometimes actually blinded that he may not be distracted from that world out of which flows a language of inspiration, which (even in the word power) the men of this world can neither equal nor live without.[1]

An aberrant individual type, therefore, who deliberately retained consciousness with the non-sensory world would be of sufficient social value that, despite his incapacity to yield an economic contribution, he would be retained. The

[1] The specialization of a type of visionary may indeed go back to the Paleolithic. Burkitt in *Pre-History* has collected evidence to show that the great cave paintings of the Aurignacian and Magdalenian epochs are probably the work of a caste of painters who traveled over great distances to serve widely distributed tribes. Their actual "sign manuals," the imprints which they made of their own hands dipped in paint, show also so frequently finger amputations that this may have been a mutilation initiatory rite setting them apart from the other five-fingered crafts and labors. Chadwick in his *Heroic Age* also points out the unique place the bard has in a Heroic society and how often like Homer he is blind.

next step would come to pass when the connection between the dimming of that insight and sexual maturity began to be noted. The blinding of a poet and, later, the castration of a boy possessed of a distinctive treble voice are common social practices. The name "fanatic" comes from those *fanaticoi*, the black-robed priests of the mother goddess Cybele, who castrated themselves in their frenzied rites. The subject is of great endocrine interest. All we can say here is that such mutilation may lead to a violent disturbance of the ductless glands which in some cases, though ending in debility, may cause a period of strange mental activity.[2] Later, it was discovered that castration was a wrong method, and the results desired were far better produced by sexual sublimation, in other words, by celibacy and sustained continence. Certainly it was observed that extrasensory powers were far more common in the prepubertal period. Hence the rise of the vestal virgins, those colleges of unmarried priestesses to be traced from Japan to Rome, of the sibyls and the pythoness priestesses, the most famous being those of Delphi.

Thus there appear such individuals, individualized to retain awareness of a pre-individual level of consciousness. Though nonsocial, they are socially valuable and, though living in society, which is becoming increasingly conscious of social obligation and interaction, themselves indifferent to this progress. They are individualists individualizing in non-self-consciousness.

It is this paradox which gives rise to the monk, *monachus*, who is a rule to himself and who reigns alone, and to

[2] That physical disaster which ordinarily leads to complete debility and collapse may in rare cases result in an endocrine reaction producing not a weakling but a giant. See the discussion of the Gadara skull from thirteenth century Christian burial sites in Greenland (Carnegie Foundation publications).

the monk's social pattern, first the "laura," the collection of hermitages, and then the convent. It is necessary to give attention to this type because it is in this highly specialized social pattern that we must look for the rudiments of the next development of natural moral law. Here we shall find the transitional phase between the Higher Law, the Law of Equity, and the Highest Law, the Law of Love. Here also we shall be able to discover the origin of the acute problems which still are demanding solution, moral problems which unless they are defined with care we have little hope ever of solving.

The Law of Equity permits the sanctioning of a culture engaged in making inventions. The foreconsciousness, absorbed with the sense world, is continually releasing new powers that upset the rudimentary moral balance reached at Decalogue level. But Equity, with its increased knowledge of the ramifications and "extra-ego" causal connections of the psyche, can, as in the case of money, actually detect and define the newly perceived psychosocial responsibilities and rules. This psychological inventiveness can balance the new materio-economic inventions.

Yet this is not enough, both for a positive and a negative reason. The positive reason is that of healthy growth, of evolution. We must remind ourselves that consciousness had to evolve. Evolution has continued in man by his mind becoming detached from the racial mind, from its limited understanding, and, indeed, from its type of perception. Detached consciousness is necessary and right if man is to rise above the animal. What is tragic and wrong is that man should become ego-obsessed. His detachment of consciousness is a means, not an end. Being detached from the racial ends of instinct he is free to become attached to the self-releasing anonymous ends of truth, love and beauty. Hence, as his consciousness advances, he will become interested in ends greater and beyond the needs of the community, i.e., the requirements of ethics. This means that he will be able to re-understand, understand intelligently and not merely intuitively, that the first part of the Ten Commandments is not merely the sanction for the really important part, the second part, the specifically social and ethical. God can and must be loved for Himself and not because He is a convenient sanction for the community's need of order. Truth, Love and Beauty are values and aims in their own right. The sanction of society and of social conduct is only one of the by-products of such service, worship and adoration. It is not worth while behaving as well as man must behave for society to remain in working order—healthy, orderly, rational, sane—if the only aim is to breed a number of healthy, comfortable, sane animals. A civilization which has no aim beyond a hygienic hedonism—the usual aim of Humanism—cannot generate enough self-control to assure the hygiene without which the hedonism goes rotten. It is not enough to say, "Who dies if England lives!" if the England—or any other nation—which demands that sacrifice can afford no heaven to the youth so slaughtered and cut off from all that life should have offered.

Hence the best people, the most socially consistent and contributory members of the society of Equity, begin to seek for a way of life as much above Equity as Equity is above the Law of Justice. They are looking for an aim in life as far beyond the specifically social goals of Equity as those goals are above the individualistic satisfactions guaranteed by the Decalogue. Men so advanced begin first to live as semi-solitary seers. Then they unite to form loose colleges. Later again there rise those organized colleges of married priests such as ran those training centers for education in the psychological and psychophysical methods of the "Mysteries." Such were shown to Strabo in Egypt and he recognized them as the places where Solon and Plato had been taught. In such cases, as perhaps also with the Levitical practice, while the priest was "canon in residence" marriage would be abstained from. There would thus be in this social pattern an alternating marriage.[3]

Finally, when such men discover that spiritual insight is increasingly aided by continence, they collect in celibate orders and monasticism has arrived.

Humanism's attacks upon celibacy, prompted by a pre-psychological prejudice, are still popular. It is, therefore, necessary to repeat that this development need not be antisocial. On the contrary, it is a development in balance of specialization, a development shown by all creatures that have ever sustained an elaborate society, and essential if man's social heredity is to keep pace with his physical heredity, for he no longer has inborn instincts and his mental heredity is now carried outside him. And this is also as necessary if his psychological knowledge is to keep abreast of his physical knowledge. For without profound integral insight physical knowledge can be pursued at least to a dangerous, society-wrecking point. But psychological knowledge, if it be sufficiently profound to be true vision, can only be sustained by those who have that purity of heart without which ultimate reality cannot be seen.

Evolution then requires specialization of means and specific varieties of social types. It also requires in such special "worker" types that they should have aims, objectives and far-sights which are social. These are essential to

[3] For a modern example of this see the rules followed by the Sufi Tekkes, *Durchgang im Derwisch Kloster*.

a society growing in powers but failing in intentions, but these aims, though social, are not reproductive nor familial. The three highly developed social animals, the bees, termites and ants, all produce classes specialized away from the simple reproductive pattern and so able to give those specific services without which complex social organization is impossible.

Man's supreme need is to have a consciousness which both perceives the visible world and the invisible world. As his attention in mastering the visible makes him blind to the invisible, he must, if his society is not to perish, generate those specialists who by abstaining from the visible can keep, for all society, contact with the invisible. This is not to say that the balance is an easy one. It is often lost. The seer loses touch with society and is lost by society —and, both he and it even more often lose patience with each other. Yet frequent loss of balance and falls do not discredit the upright position or the skill of walking, which, indeed, is no more than a way of moving by rapidly transforming what would be a series of falls into a series of advances by recovered balances.

But not only is a further specialization in seership necessary to meet man's demand for a vision of a goal greater than any socio-physical goal. This specialization in goodness and detachment, this emergence of the specific saint, is necessary to balance a rapidly growing social morbidity and malignancy. Here we come upon the "negative" reason for Equity's ultimate inadequacy.

Equity has, as a matter of fact, never quite balanced physical invention. It has made some discoveries in natural moral law, in the social ramifications of responsibility, so as to make some moral inventions to repair some of the damage done by unbalanced physico-economic finds, e.g.,

[110]

money. But Equity's knowledge of human consciousness is not sufficient to permit it to understand, and so to have the power to correct the ego itself. Equity cannot distinguish between that detached consciousness which is a right advance and that self-consciousness which is wrong. Indeed Equity shows very little knowledge of psychology. It is empirical and socially concerned, almost obsessed. It is only interested in man as a social animal and not as an evolving psyche. The great social reformers, such as Solon, seem unaware that they are confronted with a psychological problem, and think that inventions come either of themselves or through a few aberrant men. This latter is, of course, still the attitude of most Marxians toward capital and most pacifists toward war. So the great reformers who usher in Equity really wish to put the shadow back on the sundial instead of studying the gnomon and the sun.

Hence the ego, remaining unreduced, continues in its basic error; it remains absorbed in and with the sensory world. Force persists as the primary question, for sanction and authority are being continually called upon and challenged when custom is being continually upset. Force becomes increasingly physical, and hence in the end fully developed war appears. Equity tried chivalry as the answer to violence. But violence is a method, not an end, a method of force, and if there is no other quality of force, or if other forces, such as agreement, argument, moral right and magic, are all losing grip and conviction on and in men's minds, what then? We can illustrate this our historic problem in completely contemporary terms. In 1943 the late Archbishop of Canterbury answered protests against burning alive whole populations of German cities, that it would be a mistake to use too little force. What he meant was that there was to his knowledge no real and ultimate force save the utmost physical violence. If there is not, then it is hard to see why there should be retained an Established Church and its chief official be paid by the state an annual income of some sixty thousand dollars. If the side of evil is winning by evil methods, though the evil side's chief evil is not its ends but its evil means, what answer has the knight? The proto-Chinese Duke of Chou said, "Degenerate descendant though I am of thirty-two ancestors yet never shall it be recorded of a Duke of Chou that he engaged the enemy without first performing the sacred dance." And while carrying out these ancestral appeals to Heaven, he was defeated by those who dispensed with these equalizing preliminaries. The Austrian Marshal Daun, after being defeated by the young Napoleon, solaced himself by saying, "I would rather lose every battle than win one as has that young fellow." As Nurse Cavell said of patriotism, so we must simply say of chivalry, it is not enough. It can and does work fairly well as long as it is trial by battle, a "debate of arms" between men whose common level of technology gives them the same weapons with which to duel and whose common level of understanding limits them in the use of violence and cunning, so that combat is predominantly, as in the sex duels of animals, a test of courage and skill. As long as those interests which men have in common are greater than those about which they are in dispute, warfare can be a method of adjustment, not a ruin of rupture. Their underlying interests will bring them together again; they will spare a present disputant who shortly will become again a customer and co-operator.

Hence it was that Equity was found to be an inadequate answer to the first of the Five Questions—the basic question, "What is Force?" Thus we can see that it was not merely the demand to explore further the spiritual world that caused men to seek for a still higher law than the Law of Equity as the principle of their lives. Quite as much as the needs of the soul, the acute demands of the social order, the need to save ordinary mankind from anarchy, to save the race from the biological doom that awaits "intra-special" struggle, these practical issues demand greater spiritual knowledge. Spiritual power, a real psychic energy, must be found, an apt immaterial force, to balance and control the unbalanced physical energy operative when man's individualistic passions are released and armed with material inventions. A spiritual type must appear as trained in obtaining force as is the chemist, and as skilled in its exercise and employment as is the strategist.

The monastic orders attempt this. They essay the discovery and application of the Law of Love. A sentimental age naturally considers a Law of Love to be a contradiction in terms. Love should be "free," because, it is held, love is not a power of the will but an indulgence of feeling, not a devotion but an incontinence. The reason why sentimentalists always end by acting with brutality when given power is not merely that men of exhausted feelings are always callous, but also because men who treat love as a thing purely of the emotions cannot conceive that love not only can steel the will but can open and enlighten the mind. The Law of Love is then rightly called a Law and not an impulse because it is, first of all, simply a further advanced extension of that tracing of causality which first gives rise to the proto-individual's Decalogue insight into moral law and then to the wider tracings of Equity. There is no real break between the dawn of recognition of causal responsibility which in the simplest, crudest justice says,

[113]

"You did that and you must pay for it," the further enlightenment which adds, "In a degree, all of us in the group did it and we must help put you back on the rails at whatever cost to us and pain to you," and the full enlightenment which concludes, "We all did it and we must all recover what has been lost and he who sees this first will be first to start the salvage."

This is not sentimentality. On the contrary, far from being the easygoing forgetfulness of letting bygones be bygones, it digs up the deepest rootlets of the hidden ramifying wrong. Further, it not only demands of the forgiver an immense effort, for the debt exists and must be paid by someone. The forgiven must also rise by the effort made by the forgiver, and to the height of the forgiver. Justice is still done to the full. The criminal pays the uttermost farthing. The only difference from the old Law of Mechanical Justice, that which makes the difference between life and death, damnation and salvation, is that the judge pays first and the judged then follows suit.

This is the second reason why the Law of Love is Law. Beside being a causal principle discoverable by pure research into causality, it is also a matter of applied research. First we have to see that the law of responsibility embraces all of us, all humanity, and then we have to master the laws whereby we may live up to that knowledge. So the highest law, the Law of Love, the final and complete answer to the Five Questions was first attempted by those dedicated men and women who mobilized themselves in religious orders; so that in such regiments they might be the new force at the service of humanity, whose clashes the Law of Equity was increasingly failing to reconcile.

But if it is difficult to point to a secular society which actually demonstrated the Law of Equity, it is even harder to find full evidence of a religious society which succeeded for a considerable period in living out and demonstrating the Law of Love. We can say, as a historical fact, that the emergence of Taoism in China and Buddhism in India was not merely a newer teaching but a newer practice. We know that in both cases a great Order of avowed intentional living did arise and did have very great effects on mankind. Indeed in the case of Buddhism the conversion of Asoka put a monk on the throne and one who was prepared to use and did use during his reign with marked success much of the Law of Love and the force of a triumphant good will. Nevertheless these outstanding successes are temporary. We shall have to ask in Part II the question, "Can saints be mass-produced?" And, if they cannot be produced in large numbers, how is mankind, denied sufficiency of nondestructive force, not to fall back on that violence which we see destroys the user as much as him on whom it is vented?

There is no doubt, however, that we can, as we found was possible with Equity, construct the answers which are given by the Law of Love to the Five Questions.

To "What is Force?" the Law of Love says: It is the direct power of one consciousness, totally free of greed, fear and ignorance, on another. Such a freed consciousness, knowing itself to be one with the essential power of the universe, wholly attached to that supreme consciousness and loving God without any reservation, knows itself also to be one with all other individuals and loves its neighbor as itself. Hence its power is always greater, its force more apt, its initiative more ready than that of anyone less free, less mobilized, less informed, less charged.

But this apt force is only possible if all the Five Questions have been answered at the same level, in the same key. A remark made earlier may here be repeated, that the Five Questions and their answers are really one inter-actant principle, a giant molecule. That being so, all the answers must consist with one another. For example, question one must not be answered from the Decalogue level and question three from the Equity plane. We shall encounter this problem of answers mixed from different levels, of Equity mistaking itself as Love and Love relapsing, by absent-mindedness or absent-heartedness, into Equity or even Justice, when we deal with the problem and breakdown of Christendom. Here may lie the chief cause of its collapse.

The appropriate answer to the second question, "What is Property?" has therefore to be as high as the answer to the question, "What is Force?" Non-possessiveness is the essential buttress which allows good will, the selfless love of others, the force of an unstinted compassion, to be reared to its dominating height. Similarly, "What is Sex?" is sublimated also. The specialized and possessive form of love, necessary to hold a mate and raise young, is once more fused back, volatilized, into a universal tenderness and compassion. Likewise, "What is a Promise, or one's Word?" sublimates into a life utterly beyond the constriction of contracts and the delimiting of responsibility. Unlimited liability is accepted and complete ingenuousness is the only atmosphere in which such consciousness can breathe. Any subterfuge, any concealment, is impossible to one living in the interpenetrating Light of the Eternal Consciousness. Naturally, then, the final question has found its final answer. And with that the Law is finally completed and fulfilled. The fear of death is simply caused by separateness, the craving to be an ego. Overcome that and you have died and been born into the eternal life

[116]

already. You have "passed from death unto life because you love the brethren," because you love as God loves.

A being who has thus answered the Sphinx, not only finds the way open, he is a way opener. He solves not only the acute problem of force but also all those other four issues which had been feeding back their pressures of unresolved conflict until the whole of society broke down. Property and competitive trade, saving and capital, sex frustration, children with thwarted sense of security, and infantile resentments, now grown until they can project their balked revenge in slaughter on an entire civilization; cunning contracts woven round deceits deliberately framed to catch the other party; trust and honor and agreement used as masks for chicanery, a deep and repressed fear of death driving men to love destruction as a revenge upon life, that is determined to drive them from its table. Here we see the results of leaving the four questions unanswered. Their charges accumulated until the whole pressure came upon the question and problem of force, of imposition and restraint. No wonder our world has collapsed.

We must, however, turn back to the pressing questions, Has the Law of Love ever saved the world? Can it save mankind as a whole? No question is graver or needs franker facing. For it seems clear that if the Law of Love will not work no other law affords a basis of hope. One fact seems beyond controversy: the Law of Equity is not enough. Chivalry, the gentleman's code, fine as it was and noble as was its contribution to the past, apposite as knighthood once could be, no longer is adequate. Soldiering can never again be the profession of a gentleman. He can never hope to be civilization's policeman. The stakes are now too high for the moderately equipped and endowed player to keep his place at the board. The saint and the assassin face each other as the only competitors left for the office of guardian of mankind. It is possible that saints might adjust the present wild disbalance—they might not save the world for good but might check its headlong fall to ruin. It is possible that they might once more put the capsizing ship on an even keel. We have to own that we do not know and we must, in the second part of our inquiry, bring this question down to today. Here we must summarize the story so far.

Our thesis has been that evolution continued through the primates to man and in him has been through the evolution of consciousness. Through the Paleolithic epoch man evolved a social heredity to take the place of instinct, or of blind trial and error. Though, at this stage, man had no instincts, though he was gaining a consciousness detached from merely racial aims and was able to attend to much beyond the range of an animal's interest, his consciousness itself was not yet egoized. It was not split into a foreconscious exclusively concerned with the world of sense objects and a subconscious exclusively concerned with values. His life was still in unison; means and ends agreed; duty and desire chimed; the separate physiological unit could still only find his life, physical and psychical, in the community. This is the epoch of Animism when man only pereceives the world through the depth of the tribe and interprets experience only through the intuitive judgments of an unwritten, undefined tradition, received unquestioningly and indeed unawarely from earliest infancy. The Eternal Gospel is implicit because man does not at this level feel alien to nature and he unhesitatingly serves his kind. Force is our common exertion exercised through an amalgam of suggestion (magic) and muscle.

Wealth is our common stock. Sex is a force felt to center in no individual, to be contained indeed in all outer objects. Words are powers belonging to the group and affecting directly the environment. As the ego is yet to raise its barrier, behind what shall a particular person hope to hide his deceit and why think of deceiving? Death is even less possible to think about, for how can that which wholly lives know of death? Panic moments, when fear leads to flight or fight, or "freezing," leave no memory of the flash of terror.

The rise of Law is a symptom of becoming time-conscious. How else should one be able to recognize causality? The rise of justice is a symptom of egotism. Why else should one want his portion cut off and defended from the others? The Decalogue is not the Eternal Gospel but an attempt to correct an aberration from it. The true line of spiritual descent, at that level of the evolution of consciousness, would consist in being individualized but not egoized. The Decalogue does, however, show that moral causality is being recognized as a fact. And it does indicate how further aberration may be arrested, or at least further divergence be delayed, though it is helpless to cause a return to the true line of advance.

The Law of Equity, the higher perception of causality and responsibility, seen as extending beyond the individual, supersedes the attempts at a mechanic and individualized justice. The Eternal Gospel is now perceived as a Law of Life. The universe around him, the soul of man perceives as the manifestation of a righteous Creator Father who is educating His children. Do justly, but also show mercy and avoid pride. Seek communion with the Sanctioner. Walk humbly with thy God.

The Law of Love completes the cycle of Law. It is both

[119]

a Law, the service which is perfect freedom; and it is also the reconciliation of the two commandments into a unity. For man has overcome one after another his three conflicts and bridged his three chasms. By becoming psychically whole and integrated he has bridged the fissure in his own nature between the conscious ego-mind and his subconscious. By bridging the gap between himself and his fellows in a true communion, he has solved the social conflict. By bridging the chasm between himself and nature he is one with all life. He has solved the contradiction his inherent sense of creative freedom elicited by the beauty he sees, and the apparent soulless repetition which seems on examination to be the order of outer things.

The Eternal Gospel then transcends, by having wholly fulfilled, the whole idea of Law, both inner and outer. Man knows that he is free. Further, he knows now that his idea of Law, whether rigid or flexible, was, at best, a convenience for his limited, isolated mind, to help him, by perceiving and obeying law, to arrive at freedom. When man thought law inflexible it was because he was first captivated, and then captured, by an aspect, a temporary aspect, of his evolving consciousness. Those who fulfill the Law of Love lead us to see that in the vast spiral of evolution, man, in the end, returns to the primal freedom because he has been brought back to the fundamental unity.

But may we not hope that the journey signifies more than a mere salvage? Something has been eternally added to the sum of things, when that which was detached from racial consciousness and dependency was permitted to attain to freedom, to risk its isolation in egotism, to fall into and be rescued from the "I," to come willingly and

[120]

awarely to the highest and completely comprehensive attachment. Man has been freed from a blind captivity to the will of the race, so that he may choose the service which is perfect freedom, choose the supreme Meaning "in whose will is our peace." "Our wills are ours to make them Thine." Having so made them is not merely redemption but sanctification; and because sanctification is an act of the man's will who begs for it, sanctification is also creation. Temporal experience has not only recovered the Eternal, but has added to it.

PART II

The Christian Emphasis

VII

The Six Epochs of Christianity

WE HAVE now seen in briefest outline the teaching of the Eternal Gospel, the Perennial Philosophy. At first it is an intuition of man's sonship with the Life which sustains the whole universe visible and invisible and of man's brotherhood with all the other children of that Fatherhood. That intuition, later, has to be confirmed by acts of rebinding religion, and by sacraments, new affirmations and experiences of that communion, vivid enough to remind men whose growing interest in power over the outer world is making them forget the inner. Still later, as the detachment of consciousness increased, what had been a unison became a balance, and that balance had to be sustained by an organized religious system, psychological myths and dogmas. These psychological practices and rituals must be as elaborate and defined as were, at that stage, the advancing acts and crafts and rudimentary sciences of the secular material world. Even later, as man's experimental knowledge disclosed long sequences of regular recurrences in the material world, he began to trace in the inner world of his own motives, behavior and morality, moral laws analogous and complementary to the physical laws.

This discovery of law is, again, not static. From a crude individualistic justice, that first over-restricted conception of moral law made in the first spasm of individualism, man by interior and exterior insight perceives causality and responsibility to be wider than the individual and longer than a single life. Law becomes not only a larger responsibility but a more flexible instrument. Equity can speak of recovery and redemption, first perhaps, in finance, but later in respect to every one of the five commandments. If we all admit our common responsibility, we may all be saved. Nay more: we may obtain such power by this knowledge of living law as to obtain enough moral insight to make new moral inventions able to balance further new physical inventions. "Be equitable and do what you will."

Yet men discover a further need in man and a further depth in lawfulness. Equity by itself may balance invention, mere increase in physical power, and provide a good life. But if physical invention be misused diabolically by a few, what then can the many do? Whichever side wins, chivalry is defeated, if the many are compelled to resort to the diabolic means which the few challenge them to employ or perish.

Hence the law has to be explored further until there is discovered the Law of Love. The Law of Love does two things. It fulfills and completes the whole of law. By obedience, by accepting an ever larger responsibility and liability, man comes at last to the completion, the end of law. He comes back to creation: he becomes a co-creator.

Secondly, the Law of Love gives a goal to life which the Law of Equity cannot give. The Law of Equity ends with man accepting the social benefit and goal not merely as his obligation but as his reward. The Law of Love shows man that, if he will live up to its obligations, its reward is as much above the social rewards of Equity as its obligatory demands are greater. He who fulfills the Law of Love will enter here and now on his reward, because he will be brought, while still in the body, into the Eternal Life. And this reward not only offers the only reward adequate to the fully conscious being who has perceived the full extent of Law, the full ramifications of responsibility. It, also, and it alone, can give the only power adequate to cope with the diabolic violence let loose when fully conscious egos, freed from the last rigid restraints, the negative taboos, of a dying moral tradition, use material power to the utmost. Equity can only oppose limited violence to unlimited violence. So chivalry today is dismissed as utterly inadequate and inapposite. War today is in no possible way an "affair of honor" between men of honor. The soldier has lost his knighthood.

A new apt force is absolutely essential. That alone can be found and employed by those who have achieved and learned to practice the Law of Love. Nothing less will work. To work with such a power demands complete surrender to it. With such surrender the power is released and does provide the answer to unlimited violence and cunning. Thus three possibilities lie before civilization: The first is to refuse to produce such power and to perish by the physical unbalanced force which has been released. The second is to produce it sporadically; this may prolong civilization's life but keep it in constant apprehension and jeopardy. The third is to produce in contemporary terms sainthood. No reason exists why this should not be done. But no guarantee exists that it will be done. It all depends on the human will and on how many are willing to give up their lives to this, the only effective mobilization.

We must now examine in the remaining chapters how Christianity worked with these principles of the Eternal Gospel and how the Church attempted the completion and fulfillment of Law in its three rising demands of

Justice, Equity and Love. When Christianity arose in the West many issues of Law were unsolved, and some had hardly been stated. We today after two thousand years can scarcely claim even to have propounded all the problems, still less to have produced a solution. We may, however, avoid some mistakes that have arrested exploration in the past by attempting carefully to define our terms.

The first part of this book has undertaken a definition and historical illustration of the Eternal Gospel. Now we must follow the same course and define first what we may mean by Christianity. I am not here referring to the commonplace observation that all the great religions are numerically and chronologically great; they have spread wide and have lasted long because they have managed to find in their interpretations of life, something to satisfy every level of viable mankind, from the simplest truster in good luck to the highest votary whose sole desire is *fiat voluntas Tua*. I am considering the actual changing story of the Church. It is that courageous and informed theologian Von Hügel who stresses the fact that we can no longer speak accurately of Christianity as a single unchanging expression of certain principles. As Christianity as a whole gives its specific emphasis to the Eternal Gospel, so each epoch of the Christian Church has its specific emphasis. According to Von Hügel, as is natural from his specialized theological standpoint, a Modernist Roman Catholic, Christianity has had four great epochs, the Apostolic, the Patristic, the Scholastic and the post-Tridentine. He subdivides these sections into further series. But I feel that we cannot use his system though we may be helped to form our own by his insight. With our greater concern for society, civilization and extra-Mediterranean issues, we must use other categories and divisions. It is a historical fact that ancient capitals, trading upon past prestige and jealous of new growth, tend in the end to produce an unconscious but intense provincialism. I would then say that we cannot perceive the Christian contribution with any real fullness unless we see that Christianity in its history has had to meet and to answer six quite different situations and questions. Some of these situations and challenges lasted only a short while. But the effect which they had on Christianity was lasting. For the answer which the Church gave to such a temporary but pressing question became built into the word and thought patterns of Christian theology. Contrary to what might be supposed, as a historical fact a Church finds assimilation and acquisition of new information and insights easier than the elimination of findings which are no longer relevant or perhaps even mistaken.

The six situations which we can perceive, as clearly as geological strata, are as follows: Christianity was born into a generation and a locality in which the accepted cosmology and the deduced ethics were determined by Jewish Apocalyptic. This was the climate of the minds of the men whom Jesus Christ himself taught, the frame of reference of his actual listeners. This frame of mind lasted least long of all the Christian epochs. But because it was the actual setting in which during his ministry the Founder gave his message it had the greatest effect on the earliest documents. The human mind is much like adobe clay. After rain that clay is workable for a few hours. It then sets like brick, and so it stays through the whole of a rainless summer. Thus with man: the few critical years are those when men's minds are open to hear all they can of the great Master who has passed by. A mass of sayings and stories circulate in a ready market. Then the process

of canon-forming begins to take place. As a result a rigid
document remains; this cannot be altered without fracture, though it certainly and clearly contains much that
was quite topical and of local interest and, we might even
say, of accidental origin. As Streeter has pointed out in
The Four Gospels, probably not more than a generation
separates Irenaeus (born *circa* A.D. 130) and the time when
the Fourth Gospel must have been "a work of departure."
And yet Irenaeus can give as a reason for there being Four
Gospels and no more the statement that as there are only
Four Cherubim so there can only be Four Gospels. Events,
therefore, of this canon-forming period can produce much
greater impression on the canon, and therefore much
greater historical results, than later events of more importance but registering on a far more stubborn medium.

The second period appears when Christianity, leaving
its home and its localized first audience, sets out, under
what we may call the "epistolic" authors and the Fourth
Gospel, to disregard the topical Jewish problem of eschatology, i.e., the issue of the physical world's immanent
disappearance and the final judgment. The Christian
thinkers of the second half of the first century are already
aware and increasingly aware of the main spiritual issue
of the whole Mediterranean world. That was the issue, not
of a world about to end, but of the individual man's absorption in the question of his personal salvation. This he
hoped to secure by a Mystery Initiation. We have seen
that this question had been increasingly dominating the
mind of civilized man since the eighth century B.C. The
Jew was behindhand in this matter, as we see in his slow-
ness to ask the question and to answer the fifth interrogation as to life beyond the grave.

The word "mystery" is, of course, one of the most

nuisanceful words in the dictionary. We can see how thought climates change when we note that the word "mystic" once meant a man who had information so valuable that he would only give it to you if you would change your life and now that it means a fool who hasn't the courage to face life at all. While the companion word "mystery" which once meant the solving of the problem of personal salvation now means solving the problem of someone else's murder.

This second stage of Christian history lasts a little longer than the first but, in comparison with the whole history of the Church, is still very brief. It owes, in the main, its enduring power over our thought and language because it too obtained place in the canon before that canon closed forever.

The third stage's oncoming we can date from the last book to succeed in entering the New Testament canon. That complicated pseudepigraphic Apocalypse with which the New Testament is completed has been dated *circa* A.D. 95 and it shows clearly in spirit and incident the entry of the third phase. The book is so strongly apocalyptic in imagery and phrase, in story and style that still many authorities seem to think that the author must have appropriated a Hebrew Apocalypse and botched it to his specific topical need. Yet the intent of the book is clear. Christianity in its third phase is assuming a still wider role. No longer concerned with specifically Jewish thought, no longer specifically interested in the growth of Sacramentalism to meet the desire for personal salvation, the Church has now taken up the challenge and has decided to become the Opposition of the Empire. The Church is now prepared to dispute with Caesar for the headship of the world; its ringing war cry is *delenda est*

Roma. Babylon must fall. Christianity is to be mobilized to liquidate the vast secular humanism which was the Empire's *raison d'être.* The good shepherd who leads his flock beside the still waters into the Father's Kingdom, had become the shepherd who laid down his life for the flock. Next (a transition common in other soteriological religions [compare Dionysius who is both the bull and the bull-driver and Pan who is both the goat and the arcadian goat-herd]), the shepherd becomes the lamb, and the lamb sacrificed to shed his saving blood. But now the transition has to be so rapid, the extension of objective so extreme, that the lamb's nature is transformed. It is "the wrath of the lamb," not his love, before which the Empire crumbles. It is the conquering hero (of whom we may say in heraldic language that his crest carried the lamb's fleece but whose arms it is that prevail) who, with the blood of his enemies splashed up to his charger's bridle, sweeps on to annihilate his foe. Such a book must have been a trumpet call to defiance. In only one passage can we catch, amid its martial clangor, the note of appeal: "Behold I stand at the door and knock."

This third phase lasted for just over two centuries. Then, with a suddenness, the catastrophic violence of which would have startled the author of the Apocalypse more than the world's end, and with an unexpectedness for which the Church was totally unprepared, the fourth epoch broke. It was ushered in with all the violence of breaking of one of the "seals" so dramatically described in Revelation.

When violence takes place in the direction where we believe our own interests to lie, we seldom recognize it for what in fact it is. As Chadwick has said in *The Heroic Age,* a Heroic Age seen from the standpoint of the hero

[132]

gives us the *Iliad*; but seen from the standpoint—or worm's-eye view—of the conquered it gives the Anglo-Saxon Chronicle with its conclusion, after its catalogue of the "acta," the deeds of "mighty men," of physical prowess and saga reputations: "Men said openly that Christ and his saints slept."

The Church which had become inured to think of itself as the Divine Majesty's authorized permanent Opposition, the perpetual critic of the Magistrate (we have seen in Tertullian's words the Church's contemptuous reply to those who like Celsus would ask it not to secede from mankind and civilization), this Church was suddenly jockeyed off its feet, by the jujitsu of one of the most ably cynical and realistic of all those strange tyrants who inherited and vastly increased the personal autocratic power of the Principate of Augustus. With one masterly twist of policy, so cold-blooded that for an equal piece of statecraft we have to seek till 1941, he broke the back of two oppositions, or rather he threw his two serious enemies at each other's throats.

Against the endemic danger of militaro-political revolt he mobilized the Imperial Power's only other enemy, the ceaselessly vigilant and effective protest of a body which by a technique of nonviolence strike tactics carried to the pitch of what may be called "white-mail," had compelled militarism to own that it was practically helpless. Against an organism whose weight was mysticism and whose cutting edge martyrdom, a power which had only arms and torture could do as little as a man with a gun against rays which he cannot see but which deal his body cancer. The Church had the power of hitting at the cohesion of loyalty without which the master of the legions was helpless and which he himself (were this essential social cement decayed) was powerless to recreate.

It might well seem at this point then that the history of Christianity was over. Was there now any choice before it but to live officially, "happy ever after," or (the other account of the sequel) to live locked up forever after with fetters of gold? But the actual historical fact was again stranger than the expectations of either apologists or critics. Christianity was not to live the pensioned sanctioner of the armed state. It was the armed state that disappeared, in spite of the Church not only having ceased to criticize but having become the approver of its practices. The Church had thought that it was entering on a business partnership which would place it for all time above the peril and poverty of a disordered world. It had in fact married a dying partner. It rapidly found itself the inheritor of an utterly bankrupt estate.

It was at that time that what the world had taken to be Christianity's most bizarre and antisocial pattern, Monasticism, proved to be the Church's most valuable service to humanity. As has been said, for a number of centuries, Benedictinism was the answer, the only answer, to Barbarism. Beothius, the cultured philosopher who strives to serve the barbarian Theodoric, is, when the healthy savage becomes an ailing paranoic, clubbed to death for his pains. Cassiodorus is more cautious, but the work on which this administrator of the Dusk rightly prided himself was having founded two monastic houses. He saw that civilization would go on sinking still deeper, mankind having lost power of cohesion and therefore only organizations complete in themselves and able to generate their own cohesion could save themselves and having done so start saving mankind. In an inundation, before you can help others you

[134]

must yourself find a raft. Benedictine monasticism, that Rule which its great son, the Saint Pope Gregory the First, called specifically a "rule of discretion," of pre-eminent balance, was necessarily nothing less than a psychiatry, an economy and a policy. First, it was a way for men to live together so that they might have the power to rise above the psychological problems which wreck community on the rocks of temperament. Secondly, it was an economic solution so that men might find themselves self-sustaining and self-sufficing in a bankrupt and starving world. And thirdly, it was a balanced life of scholarship and instruction in all crafts and arts so that the men who were so trained might become the teachers of religion, culture and technics to a world which had lost every one of these.

Such an unsuspected success had to lead to the fifth Christian contribution. Whether the Church of the Dark Ages foresaw it or no, by the eleventh century there was no power equal to it in all the West. At the dawn of the ninth century a pope can make a chieftain emperor in order so to regularize the position of the *defensor fidei*. And we must not forget that the immediate predecessors of Charlemagne had had to intervene, depose popes and insure some kind of moral decency in the Curia when the reigning influence in Papacy had come to be called the pornocracy. In the last part of the eleventh century Hildebrand, though at the limit of his bluff, can at Canossa see the Emperor Heinrich kneeling in the snow deserted by his troops. The Pope is so certain his psychological power is greater than the sword, that he has the assurance to make the Emperor feel the depth of his humiliation. Even after a century and a half, Innocent III can give away kingdoms and restore them. This, however, is not due merely to a revival of magic, a collapse in education so great that even the most energetic men of action quail before a superior witch doctor. The display of power by the Papacy is not the real theme, nor is the papal power the real power during this epoch. The Holy See is powerful not because the Church has been the salvager of mankind and holds the power of the keys. These considerations are influential, but they compel the imagination of the common man because the mind of the intellectual has been won to reverent respect by the Church's intellectual achievement. The revived Thomism of our day does at least make many realize that the intellectual stature of the Christianity of the thirteenth century was of high quality; any history of philosophy that disregards scholasticism, just because in its decadence it became helpless and in its heyday was absorbed with nonmaterial issues, is unjust.

Here was an age when religion was unafraid of reason and disinclined to take refuge in sentiment. It openly challenged the thinking man, and raised as its apologetic a system which boldly asserted its rationalism, declared departure from reason to be sin, and was ready to present an elaborate argument (if not openly and fairly to argue) on every point of doctrine. Indeed, as so great an authority as Lightfoot maintained, the thirteenth century is the climax of that epoch, that fifth type of Christianity, when the religion of the West approached most closely to affording a complete answer to all the questions of man and the problems of society. Art, philosophy, economics; arms, laws, manners; labor, business, chivalry; ritual, dogma, mysticism: to every one of these Christendom had in those days an answer which was passably adequate, adequately reasonable, adequately workable, defensibly Christian.

That it was no more than that, we need no particular knowledge of Christianity or precise definition of the

[136]

Eternal Gospel to inform us. Christendom was then master in its own house. Pope and priest (*sacerdotium*), emperor and knight (*regnum*), business and labor—they were all ranged and rated on eternal principles in an organism coterminous with civilization. That this was a wonderful achievement we may and ought gladly to allow. But that does not compel us to accept that interpretation as final nor to maintain that the breakdown was due solely to the perversity of malcontents. True, in the thirteenth century it is possible that the Christian tradition, which had been the receiver in bankruptcy of the Roman Empire, had proved itself to be a competent receiver. Out of scanty assets it had built up with the disintegrated populations a company able to face its liabilities. But the fact of growth was not faced. The thirteenth century culture was certainly not static but, though it moved, it did not move fast enough. The living elasticity of its power of cohesion was not equal to the powers of expansion within it. It did not prove competent to meet the risk of disruption through increase of physical invention. That risk could only have been met by masterly creative parallel advances in psychological discovery. But, on the contrary, we can see an increasing tendency for the Rite (the Mass) and the Thought (the later Scholasticism)—to become ankylosed. After Aquinas has balanced the sudden centrifugal outswing occasioned by the rediscovery of Aristotle, no equal master of equilibrium appears. Hence, as Von Hügel has stressed, the later Scholasticism is as sterile and word-spinning as the earlier had been apposite. Occam's Razor shows the jungle of unreal terminology, of reasoning apart from all ratio to action, in which medievalism had lost and entangled itself.

The inadequacy of the thought system was, however, only one symptom of Christendom's failure to keep pace with the divergent growth of man's consciousness. Already, fearing that certain dogmas would be questioned, the Church ceased to argue and adopted the most terrible form of violence and cunning. Dominic, who starts out assured that reasoned preaching must convince, cries, with an impatience more sinful and more punished than Moses': "I have given you reason: now I shall use force." Bonaventura may still so believe in reason's gentle power that he can write: "A population grows up far more irreligious if it has the sacraments but no preaching, than one who has preaching but lacks sacraments." The fact remains that the Inquisition, the Holy Office, steadily spread, an institution which outraged every principle of justice, not to mention mercy. In its tribunals the accused could have no defender, nor was he confronted with his accuser; not only was torture regularly used but for the accused to deny his guilt was for him to be condemned.[1] Secret in its methods, appallingly cruel in its means, the use of such an institution branded the hand that wielded it. And as always happens when resort is had to an evil method, violence led to counterviolence which again was used to justify more violence. We who are involved in a similar descent cannot cast stones at such bewildered and frustrated good men, for (and herein lies the heart of the tragedy) many of these very officers of scientific cruelty were, personally, men of the highest self-discipline. The last pope to be canonized is Pius V. He was a man of intense rectitude in his private life, of deep and selfless devotion to his religion and his office. At the beginning of the seventeenth century, men were not lightly made saints, "raised to the altar." Yet he was raised to the chair of St. Peter, straight from the chairmanship of the Inquisition itself, by such outstandingly

[1] See H. C. Lea, *History of the Inquisition.*

good electing cardinals as St. Carlo Borromeo, and his conduct as pope was so completely in accord with his procedure as Grand Inquisitor that Ranke in his *History of the Popes* can say that with him at last the Inquisition is crowned head of the Church.

Inevitably, then, Christianity enters its sixth phase as desperate opposer of progress, and is itself rent within. Its answer to the next great problem, what we may call the emergence of the post-Aristotelian world, is not an answer but a denial. When the French king can actually sequester the pope so that the successors of Hildebrand and Innocent, who had tamed emperors and had tributary kings, now live under the control of the military ruler of a single sector of Europe, then society is being prepared for the disintegrating scandal of the great schism which in turn ends with the final fissure of Christendom. The North in that case seceded from the South; and Protestantism and Roman Catholicism divide Christianity. This means more than that there are two Christianities in open and irrepressible competition. What is worse is that neither of these Christianities is any longer a complete answer to life, a complete complement and balance to material progress. Catholicism tries to stop that progress. Protestantism, on the other hand, endeavors to keep religion from impeding that progress. As we shall see, when we trace the play of the three lawful expressions of the Eternal Gospel during these six epochs of Christianity, physical progress after the Reformation becomes revolutionary while psychical progress actually goes into reverse. Expansion advances by geometrical progression but cohesion regresses almost as fast. This is unmistakable when we look at any series of historical maps of Europe. There we see that Europe, which is split in two in the sixteenth century, after a brief attempt to become a

[139]

Protestant North and a Catholic South, becomes by the end of the seventeenth century a series of absolutely independent nations acknowledging no moral overlordship. These nations, however, though far smaller than medieval Christendom, are far too large to awake permanent loyalty in their constituents. Hence, though the nineteenth century is the century of economic expansion it is just as truly the century of psycho-political contraction. The nations of the eighteenth century were fairly "viable." That is to say, they were balances or congruences between areas large enough to correspond very nearly to the economic powers of their inhabitants, and areas small enough not to be well beyond the embrace of the loyalty-capacity of those inhabitants.[2] The nineteenth century sees economic power increase until all Europe is far too small as an efficient economic unit, while, *pari passu*, psychological starvation waxes so acute, the power of cohesion, the spontaneous sense of loyalty so weakens and shrinks, that nation after nation splits and sunders and splits again. In the nineteenth century in North America democracy denied secession: in Europe it acclaimed it. And in those nations, wherein physical progress is most rapidly advancing, this fatal fissuring is most constant. Spain, a reactionary power, loses its empire, but as a nation hangs together. The Low Countries sunder, and in turn Belgium splits into Walloons and Flemings. Norway splits from Sweden, as had Finland before; and in consequence Scandinavia is now a prey for states lower in physical life-standard, but higher in psycho-social cohesion. The United Kingdom loses Ireland; and

[2] For example, France was for a period an area large enough to give adequate scope to the economic expansion then possible and yet not so large that intense devotion could not be felt for the whole country.

[140]

Scotland would be able and willing to extort a large measure of independence, were it not that the Highlanders desire to secede from the Lowlanders.

Meanwhile there appear, as well as these vertical fissures, horizontal fissures. Europe is laminated by class loyalties and class wars. This adds to the anarchy because these lateral divisions forge no true ties that will hold across frontiers. They simply split the nation another way. Thus in one small area there may be not only several groups acknowledging no common moral law with their neighbors, but living in latent civil war with those above and below them. The Tower of Babel not only defies every other tower; each tier in each tower is in dispute with every other floor.

This small excursion into politics is necessary because almost no attention has been paid to this supreme problem, the problem of psychosocial cohesion. All trust has been put in economo-political increase—raising the physical standard of life—and expansion backed by arms. Yet as definite a balance exists and must exist and must be maintained between these two as between the explosive power of a gas and the tensile strength of its container. Gas energies cannot be employed unless metallurgical knowledge gives proportionate cohesive power. Our society is wholly devoted to making social explosives and undertakes no research into social containers and cohesives. When the container cannot endure the expansion, our one cure is to repair the rupture with a further use of explosive power— with more violence. You cannot contain one explosion with another.

That is the reason for the otherwise inexplicable phenomenon of countries, most advanced and advancing in those economic powers which demand whole continents

[141]

in which to function fruitfully, being the very same countries which continually split politically into less and less politically viable units. Owing to his obsessional interest in economic expansion and physical power, man is so psychosocially ignorant that all he can do is to retreat faster and faster in his desperate search for a basis of consent, a container and circuit of cohesion.

That is the reason why religion must be brought back as the chief interest and concern of our lives. For only by religious understanding, only by a keen interest in and a wholehearted exploration of the whole psyche, and of those vast invisible areas to which it is the bridge, can we hope to make those discoveries in dynamic cohesion that will permit us to use without destruction the physical powers we have unleashed.

Psychology as at present practiced is not enough. Like the Decalogue Law of Justice, psychology can only recognize the working of law up to the frontiers of the individual. It is not enough to say that you have made the root discovery of a man's maladjustment to his life when you have uncovered some deep personal and repressed conflicts. These have been a cause of his failure in outward relationships, but these causes may be themselves only effects, epicentral disturbances produced by shocks taking place in the world around the patient. If we are all in touch with one another beneath the threshold of individual consciousness—and of this there seems now no reasonable doubt to any who choose to investigate the question of extrasensory perception—then how can we deny that, as we are all linked, we are subject to strains which only a much ampler psychology than we have at present could calculate, still more relieve. Psychology must take the world as its parish before its anthropological knowledge and approach will be adequate. So conceived, I dare prophecy, psychology will have become unmistakably religious. It will have come to recognize the significance of social heredity, the existence of various members and types in the body politic of mankind[3] and it will indicate and assert the essential value to the body politic of the seer type, the eyes of that body. Psychology must recognize that its task is to render in contemporary terms all that profound and essential psychological knowledge encysted now in dogmatic terms. When it has done that, it will find in its hands the contemporary rendering of the Eternal Gospel.

Certain it is that any maintenance of our present economic powers, let alone any further progress in them, depends on our finding their psychological equivalent and balance. If we fail to realize this balance, then we face only two choices. Either we shall have a complete collapse of our civilization, for man will have at his disposal ever more physical violence and ever less consent and loyalty. Or there must ensue a rapid recession and secession in group living until men find themselves back at the level where consent is once more spontaneous, uncoerced. That level is now so vestigial—we have left in us so little natural cohesion, spontaneous loyalty is at such low ebb—that its economic equivalent is probably somewhere near the economic standards, skills and standard of life of a Bronze Age tribe.

[3] See Dr. William H. Sheldon's *The Varieties of Temperament.*

VIII

The Division of the Counsels and the Precepts

WITH this skeleton outline of two thousand years of Western history before us, we can see how the six epochs of Christianity illustrate the Christian emphasis on the Eternal Gospel. We have seen that if we are to estimate that Christian contribution we must judge it, in each phase, with regard to whom, to what situation, the Church was offering its answer.

In stages one and two those who were winning a hearing for their interpretation of "God's Good News" are addressing individuals not societies. Much as the approach to an apocalyptically-minded Jew and a mystery-minded Greek might differ, these two openings had one thing in common: the present world was a doomed failure and man's duty to his neighbor as much as to himself was to find the way into the new order, the new age, the new life. Now the ethic which this demands has, of late, been dismissed as an interim ethic; and ethics which are only for a specific and passing emergency are, what one might call in modern vernacular, concentration camp codes of conduct. They are practical findings, answers to the pressing problem how best to endure wholly unnatural conditions of arrest. It is clear that such advices can have nothing to do with an Eternal Gospel, for they do not attempt to answer any of the Five Interrogations or to trace the Five Causalities. Force, possession, sex, a man's word and death: men restrained from

[144]

living in the world cannot pronounce on these. The first is wholly in the hands of others, the second wholly at their mercy, the third wholly frustrated by them, the fourth unaccepted by them and the fifth made wholly incalculable by them. As was said by a man of high intelligence, integrity and strength, who survived such an experience with a rare detachment, the only way to endure in a concentration camp is to abandon every shred not only of expectation but of trust in causality and live a life of instant adaptability to an utterly irrational irrelevance. But we have seen that the ethic as crystalized in the Matthew Gospel as the Sermon on the Mount is not a system which mocks system, a series of paradoxical gestures of defiance such as Prometheus might have hurled at Jove. On the contrary, it is a rational tracing of causality. Indeed it is more causal, a more thorough and drastic tracing and elucidation of natural moral law than was the legalism of the Decalogue or the socialism of the codes of Equity. Where they each in turn stopped short the great masters of detection and deduction, such as the Buddha and the Christ, had tracked the threads of responsibility back to their sources and so at last and alone had given to those, who would follow these lines, the clue, the way, the truth, the life.

Though the ethic of the Sermon on the Mount is not an interim ethic, it is, however, a radical ethic. It starts at the very base, at the final roots of action, the individual's will. Though it is not a mere *ahimsa,* a negation and an abstinence, a refusal to do anything, a determination just "to hold one's breath till the bang lets loose the cheering," it is a resolve to take first things first and to find that "first" at a base far earlier than the ordinary man thinks of beginning. This starting so imperceptibly early, this beginning with the seed, when current morality was calling for axes

[145]

and tree felling, may be said to be due to an occasion and a cause. The occasion was the actual situation from which the Christian Gospel emerged. Jew and Levantine Greek then had, we have seen, in common an individualistic attitude to religion. The Jew had been so often beaten that his one social hope lay in a divine cataclysm. He could prepare his soul for the Day of the Lord, but it was the Lord and the Lord alone who would usher in that divine event. The Levantine Greek had not yet recovered from his crushing by the Roman Power. Sometimes it is forgotten that Aristotle is right about actual empires. Like Hitler's and Napoleon's, Ghengis' and Alexander's, their time span is somewhere between ten and twenty-five years. Our failure to recognize this is largely due to the Roman Empire. But as a historical fact it follows the same rapid course. The Augustan Principate takes on the full imperial features only with Tiberius, and the advisers of his second successor, Claudius, have already gone far to reverse the process and create an *ad hoc* federalism (to the disgust of the imperialistic Juvenal) by extending the sacred citizenship of the victorious Roman to anyone, regardless of blood, who lives as a free and successful man within the vast administrative areas. Hence the Greek world to which Paul preached was far more sorry for itself, far more hopeless of any social future worth having, than the Greek world, say, of Origen. Christianity then can begin with the Law of Love. As we have seen in the evolution and definition of the Eternal Gospel, in the tracing of the moral law's causal connection, the Law of Love is a final term, a completing of a slow exploration, a culmination.

In Christianity the process is reversed, and the last is first. It starts by making its appeal to men who have individually seen much sorrow, who have seen their hopes of political and any large scale amelioration utterly defeated, who want, above all, the ending of sorrow and who see, if that sorrow is ever to end, they must end it in themselves and for themselves. But when we allow that, we must at the same time guard ourselves against assuming that because Christianity started and starts with individuals and with their spiritual problem, their psychological difficulty, Christianity is thus shown to be simply a religion of private salvation and other worldly solutions. A man's own salvation and the world's salvaging are not incompatible. Rather, it is only by saving men right down into their subconscious and right on beyond death and their fear of it, that you may, in the fire of such a redemption, bake man's soft soul into bricks of such endurance that they may sustain the vast crushing pressures of the walls of the *Civitas Dei*.

It seems doubtful, however, if the subapostolic age realized the full implications of this fact. We must recall that the Church, by the close of the first century, is not only itself going through a bewilderingly rapid growth. Its Jewish-Messianic Apocalypticism is being left behind: it is already mainly talking Greek to Greeks. The Messianic aspect of Christ's ministry is being eclipsed by the aspect of him as the saviour Sacramental God. Beside the change within the Church, the world it is addressing is changing too. The writer of the Apocalypse is not, as he thinks, closing an age but finishing a literature. It is Apocalypticism that died, not the Empire whose death the Revelation prophecied. The Empire took on a new lease or rather a new life. The Greek world found that it had a stake in civilization, and so completely did the Greek recover, that it is John of Cappadocia who crowns Roman Law and it is in and through Greek Byzantium that the Roman Empire,

[147]

for a whole millennium extinct in the old robber's nest by the Tibur, continues until, in 1453 as it falls, the Middle Ages are over, the medieval Church and Empire are over and the modern world has begun.

The Church then had an immense choice before it, but, sadly, it must be owned, only small and reactionary men were there to take it. The Revelation is not a book morally fit to close a canon that opens with the book which contains the Sermon on the Mount. But quite as important as is the tone of the Apocalypse, is its sociological and cosmological outlook. It is looking back not forward. True, it is the first social or sociological work which the Church produced. Right up to Peter II the Church is still confining its message to individuals and its sole social advice is "Serve God: honor the king," obey the magistrate as appointed by God and given the sword of justice as his rightful instrument. With Revelation, however, the Church has a social program and platform, and the program is one of organized opposition. The final contribution of Greek social philosophy had been the stoicism of Zeno, as enlarged by Cleanthes and Chrysippus. The Roman general who had put on the toga of the forum met the Greek philosopher who had become the magistrate. The new Empire of law citizenship was born of this union. Hence Revelation's prophecy was falsified—the Empire did not fall, even in the West, for another ten generations. In this reconstitution of Hellenic-Roman civilization the Church was offered a part. Gibbon's well-known phrase, "To the magistrate every religion was equally useful," is true, if taken with the latent sneer unsounded. As the emperor Alexander said when he placed the statue of Christ and Moses in his private oratory, "Every religion which would teach men to be better should be reverenced," a saying which echoes the great edict of

[148]

Asoka. The Church, however, refused to co-operate. It went back to the Jewish hope of a supernatural destruction of everybody save the chosen people. The issue it fought upon was closely parallel to that raised today by Jehovah's Witnesses, the refusal to make an act of loyalty to the social symbol. It is interesting to note that today the Church of Rome has ruled that in China Confucius may be reverenced and saluted as a patriarch and that this act of national reverence is compatible with the strictest orthodoxy. The question of idolatry was one which the Church at the turn of the first century is regarding far more in a literal than in a spiritual sense. It is, as the Apocalypse shows, looking back to that Judaism, which, having banned image worship, fancied it was delivered from idolatry and, proud of its supposed victory, fell into the idolatrous error of worshiping the letter, until the superstitiously reverenced letter killed the spirit. That spirit of pseudepigraphic editing and authorship, which sails so close to forgery, need not be considered as utterly discrediting a writer, but it must be taken into account when estimating the climate of truthfulness to which such authors felt they had to conform. We may ask, which was the more idolatrous: to conform with custom, and social solidarity and give a pledge of service and citizenship by a conventional salute to a political symbol? or to treat ancient writings with such superstitious awe that, even when they deny the spirit of the gospels, they are held to be inspired? Is not the real idolatry to worship an ancient name so blindly that not only must any author who would issue a new message pretend that it is an old pronouncement, but by so doing he may succeed in claiming as inspired a teaching which, if judged by its spirit, would be self-condemned as unchristian?

Those questions are raised by the close of the first

century. (They are still demanding answer in the middle of the twentieth.) What does become clear as we continue to trace Christianity's exemplification of the Eternal Gospel is a double event: Christianity has come out into a world which has not ended. Whether the Church makes terms with society as a whole or refuses to do so, the Church itself is no longer simply a body of individuals seeking personal salvation. The Church has become a society. In modern language Christianity has ceased to be purely and only a psychiatry. Whether it will become a policy, whether it will have a social program in the world or whether it will continue to say No—this question as to its attitude to that third term of human activity was still undecided. But the Church has, inevitably, moved into the second term that lies between the individual's concern with his own interior conflict (the psychiatry which heals him) and the concern with mankind in its largest units (policy, the methods of government). That second term is, of course, the economy.

The results of this are very serious, demanding rethinking of problems to which the Church's individualistic stage of psychiatry gave no answer because such problems were not on its horizon. We may ask again, Did the subapostolic thinkers and administrators realize their situation? We have seen that the Synoptic teaching is individualistic. It must begin by being so: First and most obviously, because of its occasion, the conditions under which the preaching was actually begun, a teaching addressed to a people not merely un-enfranchised but relieved of all their political responsibilities, save those of paying taxes and appearing in alien law courts. But there was in addition sound cause for so beginning. Alter a few units completely, cause a few seeds to mutate, make a few grains of the vast mass of inert matter radioactive, and these few could inaugurate a new age. They would be leaven in the lump—a living culture, a new breed. These few, however, must be nothing less than that; they must be changed not merely in conduct or even in character but in consciousness. They must have passed from this life which is a death into the Eternal Life. With these few, who fulfill the Law to the utmost limit of Love, society is leavened. The whole loaf will not become a solid mass of yeast. But the whole of it will be raised, aerated, inspired, not so much by contagion with, but expansion from, the power which the minute living yeast cells, through their ferment, can transmit to the otherwise inert dough.

Did the disciples understand? For example, Peter, Peter who could be prepared to believe that the deaths of Ananias and Sapphira were due to psychic powers delegated to him. Was Peter himself a transmuted consciousness living wholly and unwaveringly in the Law of Love and so able to have the highest answer to the question, "What is Force?"

True, the Church does try to enter on an economy of the highest kind. The early days of the Christian Society in Jerusalem saw an attempt at collectivism. Certainly collectivism requires that every individual member be a practicer of the Law of Love, if the collectivism is not to vanish, as did the attempt at Jerusalem in a few months. This collectivist phase clearly did break down. Further, we know from Paul's practical provisional advice that he found many in the new Church who were content to be parasites. His words, "He that will not work, neither shall he eat," are plain proof of that. We can have no doubt that many individuals in the churches were not functioning at the level of the Law of Love. Indeed we may doubt whether many had attained even to the Law of Equity, for a society

[151]

of gentlemen will not find as a serious issue the problem of what to do with those who under the guise of fine words wish to live at their fellows' expense.

It is such considerations as these and further information on the same matter that can leave us in little doubt that quite early, perhaps by the last quarter of the first century, the Church had made a further important discovery. Though the division was only explicitly stated later, still by the second generation Christianity had begun to realize that it was made up of at least two levels of people. To the higher, to those who accepted the Synoptic standards, pertained the Law of Love. But this level of Law was not universal, it was not obligatory in anyone who would be saved: far from it. The majority, it was undeniably obvious, would never rise in this life to such a height. So the Law of Love comes to be known not as a Law but as counsel of perfection. To attempt to make a large number of individuals, who had joined up for multifarious reasons, all conform with the highest standard, was clearly vain. To trust them to do so was simply to invite disruption. They would become hypocrites in their private lives, and, in their social relationships, parasites. A secondary code, a code of minimum and really essential conduct, the Precepts, to break which was to lose salvation—these lowest level rules must be added as a base line of conduct. Then if these were broken, the offender must be excommunicated.

This compromise was unavoidable and we cannot say that in the circumstances it was wrong. Christianity had reached its third stage. In the first two its message was confined to individuals who were prepared to give everything and to change everything to attain salvation—first in the new life which was to come upon the world at any moment, and next in the life which everyone must enter after death. Such individuals of these first two stages had been shown how that salvation might be attained, what it was and what it required of them. The way was narrow, the gate narrow and few found it. Those that did yielded everything, were sold out because they had bought the Pearl, had left father and mother, and wife and children. In the third stage the message of the Church was to whole classes. There had to be room for two divisions. First came those who heard and, in a moment, with a sudden conviction, knew that they had found the goal of their lives, knew that they had come upon what they had always been blindly seeking and for want of which life, whatever it gave, could never satisfy. They knew that their consciousness had mutated—they were altered right through by the *metanoia*, the change of their basic being. But there also had to be room for "trainees," for catechumens, people only prepared to change slowly and to put no date when they would come to a total commitment. Beside the few on fire with the love of God and of man for God's sake, consumed with one passion, the passion of the apostolate, there had to be a place —a large place—for men in whose lives salvation had an important meaning but not the only one, who wanted the Eternal Life but all in due time, who wanted God, but first of all with "His gifts and not for Himself." These meanwhile, therefore, wanted the temporal life as well with family and householding and much pleasure in actual living. Their hunger for God had been satisfied with the promise that one day it would be filled. The pang was not so keen that it could not be assuaged with a promise.

The Church had ruled that none who joined her could take the part of a citizen in political life. All the more, therefore, a specific economy had to be worked out for its members. The Sermon on the Mount might be followed as an ethic in the home. Many families always interiorly live a much higher morality than their constituent individuals succeed in living in society at large and in their businesses. But the issue here was: Could the Sermon on the Mount serve as an ethic between large accumulations of families, all bound by the fact that they had just been admitted to Church membership?

If we are to take the Pauline Epistles as a reliable description of mid-first-century Christian life, the answer is probably No. The apostle has to chide Christians for taking one another into the pagan courts. The passage in the Gospel of Matthew, about expelling members who repeatedly break the rules, may well be an interpolation into the original teaching, but, again, it probably reflects conditions and difficulties familiar by the latter part of the century. In short, it became clear that though Christianity had started at the top of the Law, now it must, if it was neither to convert the whole world to the Law of Love nor desert the world by ending all social and family life, create a ladder of stages whereby the world might climb by degrees and at its own pace to the final station. And even if the world refused to climb, was it not an achievement to have raised a large mass above flood level? We must always remember that the Church was answering two different questions at the same time: first, How may one find God? and secondly, How may one escape damnation? These questions are not identical for most people.

The real problem of the Sermon on the Mount, then, is not whether it is an Ethic of the Interim, that is, an ethic for everyone who would be saved, but an ethic only for a moment, only to be able to be practiced during a pause in history. The question rather is whether it is a "selective

[154]

service" ethic for all time, giving essential benefits to all indeed, but to be practiced seriously by a few picked volunteers alone, inducted, for the sake of the rest, into permanent mobilization.

It would seem, then, that this was the obvious occasion when from the height of the Law of Love would be let down, for men on a lower level, that stage from which, as we have seen, man had ascended to the Highest Law. Surely Equity was precisely this standard now required by a religious society which lived together with a higher respect for one another and more mutual responsibility than was required by individualistic justice, yet with less than required by the Law of Love? Indeed I venture to think we may say that Equity is par excellence the Law for those societies wherein economics is the paramount activity and interest. In a society where psychology is recognized as giving the profoundest interpretation of man, there that society will show that, as man's interresponsibility and his interdependence are only coterminous with mankind, the Law of Love is the only Law which actually covers the case. Where politics is considered the only real estimate of human relations, there the Law of Justice, the *Lex Talionis*, the arbitrament of the sword, and the conception of individuals as each separate and each wholly responsible for his own acts, is the view of life. In the middle condition, where men trade but do not have to govern, enter into contracts and partnerships but do not attempt to understand one another beyond the demonstration given by financial advantage, where they breed but do not intend to war, there Equity rules. As we shall see, in a specifically economic age, such as the nineteenth century, the Law of Equity is present and dominant in most men's minds. And this Law finds its specific expression so strongly in the eco-

[155]

nomic panel of the Five Answers, in the answer to the question, "What is Wealth? What is Property?" that the nineteenth century's great invention may be said to be co-operation, a word confined specifically to business dealings, to economic activity. We may add that this interest in trade and this belief in its paramount importance was so great as to become naïf. The attempt to explain all wars, and indeed all history, as being due simply to economic motives was one of the ignorant convictions of the nineteenth century, one at which the next period will laugh as lightly as Marxianism in its heyday laughed at those who strove to find in politics the meaning of history.

The early Christian Church had, on the one hand, no responsibility for magisterial force, or for the keeping of the frontiers against the barbarians. It had refused to co-operate with the state. But, on the other hand, it was committed to family life, to trade and to business. Origen can say with assurance that the Christians were no withdrawers from life "like the holy men in India" and he might have remembered to add also the example of the interesting though extinct agricultural subsistence experiment of the Essenes near the Dead Sea. There is then no manner of doubt that the Church was in the world, only denying co-operation on specific points, of which points business was not one of the excepted activities.

What actually happened was not an accommodation to the level of Equity but a relapse to that of individualistic Justice. This seems to have been due to two causes springing from a common root. We have seen the Church retreating, in its search for an external authority, to a doctrine of inspiration that prefers trusting the letter (and even the most dubious signature) rather than the spirit. This would mean and did mean that the Decalogue would be the only possible alternative if the Sermon on the Mount had to be provided with a second-best behavior pattern. The Decalogue was out-of-date in a world of complex contracts, of money, capital and interest. But it was "verbally inspired," and, to those whose idea of inspiration was still tied to verbalism, that settled the question. The second reason for the Church's inclination to revert to a harsh legalism when love proved too high a standard for the ordinary convert, was, what we have already seen, its growing spirit of intransigence. The Church would not attempt to understand the problems of a society coterminous with civilization but, calling itself a chosen people, destined to be saved as a remnant from the total destruction of all the rest, wished to disown common responsibility and to cultivate a spirit that would justify uncompromising defiance.

This is made unmistakably clear when we take note of the three ranks of "Church nobility" as they emerge in the subapostolic Church. When apostles are no more and prophets are being discredited, the three degrees of importance stand out and are seen to be three stages of social secession and defiance. Already in the Apocalypse, the conquering Lamb has, as his special bodyguard, virgins. This, of course, does not mean specifically females. It means those who have taken a vow against marriage. Abstinence from conjugal relationships and the family is being honored with high respect. The chief honor is, of course, martyrdom. The middle term, Confessors, emerges a little later, Confessors being those who have "witnessed," by acts of passive resistance, or denial, only stopping short of being put to death. It is worth recalling that the one ruler in English history who attained to this level of Church honor, Edward the Confessor, the last Saxon king, owes his title to the fact, not that he suffered actively for the faith, but that having married he never had congress with his wife.

Thus the series is complete: those who abstain from home life and procreation, those who protest against the state until they suffer and those who throw down their bodies as a final gage of battle. The difficulties in which such a standard of virtue was to land the Church are too familiar to need recounting. To lay down one's life is not, necessarily, to be able to live a life worthy of being offered to God. Men of notorious living actually thought to expiate all their sins by such an act, for the Church unwisely ruled that martyrdom conferred plenary absolution. What, however, made the Church finally curb such an excess was when martyrs under capital sentence proceeded to give absolution to other sinners. The blood of the martyrs may be one of the seeds of the Church, but one of its fruits is also the Inquisition.

All we need say here is that this ranking according to the degree to which a churchman defied and seceded from the state, proved, in fact, a mistaken classification. Natural moral law, the principles of the Eternal Gospel, the Five Interrogations, are not so explicated and answered. This is no discovery of Humanism. The Church itself very quickly found out the inadequacy of its first ratings in respect to ecclesiastical honors. The discovery was made as soon as the Church ceased to be simply an opposition party and had to find answers to life and not simply contradictions to Caesar. Nor must we forget that the Church had ceased to be purely an opposer and denier long before Constantine overcame her last vestiges of intransigence by his offer of partnership. That, as we have seen, made little difference to history. Rome fell and Christian Rome was, we must never forget, scarcely distinguishable in oppressive cruelty from pagan Rome. The Gladiatorial Shows continued: slavery in its cruelest form (of the *latifundia*), the torture of witnesses in the law courts as part of procedure to obtain evidence, punishments of revolting cruelty (for twelve offenses Roman Law, so praised by people unacquainted with its details, inflicted the ghastly punishment of burning alive), all these blots on any state which would claim the name civilized, still more Christian, went on under the auspices of the Church.

The real departure, the real emergence of social thinking began when the Church found that secession from society is not synonymous with secession from the world. The distinction became clearest to those who went farthest in attempting to kill the two birds with one stone. For it was in the development of monasticism that the Church raised, though it never wholly solved, the social and the economic issue, and called in, though it failed to recognize, the Law of Equity as an alternative to the Law of Love.

IX

The Mistake of Monasticism

THE monk, as his name shows, is in origin a solitary, one whose sole concern is to solve the individual psychological problem by the Law of Love. Having done so he is free either to wander through the world teaching the Liberation and Enlightenment which he has found, living on the alms which those whom he teaches may give, or he may attempt the direct action of benefiting others by prayer alone. Now that extra-sensory perception and influence can be statistically established, we are compelled to revise the Rationalist's unquestioning contempt for Contemplation. But we may still maintain that those who live solitarily may relapse into looseness and laziness and those who beg from others, because they claim that they are too busy teaching for them to be able to work, may be idlers. Certainly Church history will support such a finding, though it will also show that, with proper safeguards of selection, it may be a true social economy for an expert teacher to be excused from manual toil so that he may give more fully his specific service.

If we, out of hand, condemn any teacher's living by alms then we should have to close all the colleges. Alms are alms whether given by a rice farmer putting a handful of grain into the preacher's bowl or by a giant monopolist putting a heap of bonds into a university treasury. We say *pecunia non olet*, and we may indeed often need to be happy in the hope that money is supposed to carry less taint of its origin and danger to its user than would contaminated rice. Certain it is that the Church found that the monk, who set out to rule himself only by the Highest Law of the two commandments, could not always, indeed could hardly ever, attain at one bound to such a height. He would have to recapitulate mankind's progidal's-return from individualism. He must learn right community with a like-minded fellowship, before it would be safe for him to attempt to take the world as his parish or to strive to become mankind's voice of intercession before God.

Hence we have first the Greek "laura," the cluster of anchorites' cottages round a common Church, and, finally, and fairly soon, the common house. We must also remember, to the honor of the common sense of Christian Conventualism (and common sense is perhaps the last of eulogies that a defender of the Thebaid would stress), that the Desert Fathers set themselves against idleness and begging, utterly. Everyone had to work at weaving baskets every working day until he had produced enough economic output that its sale in the market would give him his daily bread. This pattern of living reaches this economic level just at the time when the Church becomes the partner of the Empire. As Christianity as an organization accepted the state, greater numbers deserted it. The bishops saw to the distributive end of the trade. This rule depended on a double insight, on recognizing that interdependence of economics and psychology which always exists in a sane livelihood. Man is a social individual, neither a solitary nor a fused mass. In a sane condition the work which makes him socially valuable and gives him an adequate economic subsistence is also the work which keeps him psychophysically exercised and content. Of necessity, therefore, a

[161]

society which takes the psychophysical benefit and pleasure out of economic work has, if it is to remain sane, to put it back again by organized games. And the more the economic activity becomes specialized below any craftsman's satisfaction in it, below any play of skill, the more games must become skillful, professionalized, no longer idle and careless play but proficiently earnest. For man's sanity is at stake.

If, however, there is to be a group of men trading in the world they become inevitably a corporation. How that development would have proceeded we may best judge by the order of St. Basil, the one great monastic order of the Greek Orthodox Church, and so the Conventual institute which had to make its articles of agreement with the Eastern Empire. More interesting to us is Western monasticism. Indeed it is a clearer illustration of the re-emergence of the Law of Equity to supplement the Law of Love. The earliest monasticism in the West is purely Eastern. Twelve Egyptian monks of the sixth century are buried at Clonmacnoise in western Ireland. The Thebaid was influencing Ireland by the close of the fifth century though Patrick had only founded Armagh in 444.[1] There can be little doubt that the ascetical intensity of Celtic monasticism is oriental. St. Bridget is called the Mary of the Celts, so highly did the Irish Church rate her; and her rule has been called the Rule of the Rod, so strongly does it stress flagellation as an aid to perfection. It is this type of intense and almost antisocial religious discipline that many Irish missionaries brought back across Europe. Lonely eagles of evangelism, they beat up against the heavy clouds of barbarism pouring in from the darkened East. Of these the most successful in prestige and penetration is Columbanus, called of Bobbio, for far in south Italy, deep down in that

[1] See Professor J. B. Bury's *St. Patrick.*

[162]

Mediterranean from which his desert teachers had come, this man from the green island in the North Atlantic left his weary and reverenced bones. But though the victory of his idea seemed assured by his devotion, and though the Celtic monasticism which sought only a psychological solution seemed to have linked up with its parent, the Greek Orthodox "laura," it was not so to be. The genius of Benedict is a Western parallel of the genius of another religious founder who was also born a noble. Both Gautama and Benedict passed through that phase of intense physical mortification at which Celtic and Thebaid monasticism remained. Both of them renounced such violent and risky methods for a discipline far more skilled. Both founded orders which changed history over their respective world areas. Both orders give rise to a culture based on spirituality which flowered in all the arts. In the emperor Asoka we find a man who has been a successful warrior becoming a monk and yet as a monk ruling his empire in peace and by peace. With Gregory the Great, saint, doctor of the Church, pope, wielding political power in the capital of the world which the emperor had deserted, sending his missionaries to save and recultivate the northern provinces sunk in barbarism—we have a son of St. Benedict. It is this master of many powers and arts who, as we have seen, tells us that Benedict's rule is so great because it is so discreet, that is to say, it is so balanced and adequate to meet the whole nature of ordinary men and the actual problem of a society bankrupt not only psychologically but economically and politically.

Thus the middle term of Equity emerges. On the one hand was the lofty loneliness of the solitary saint concerned with Eternity, concerned to show anyone who will, the narrow way thither. But he had a compromise to proffer the man hopelessly compromised with the world of time. The saint could fulfill the Law of Love but he could not show the masses how they could fulfill that Law. And we must ask again, can saints be mass produced? As a historic fact, is not sanctity, that fulfills the highest law, as rare as those biological mutations that do occur but occur about once in a million? On the other hand were the masses, now driven so low that many of the Dark Age societies were—as is so much of our own today—well below the Decalogue level of the Law of Justice. Benedict invented a middle society which could uphold the standard of Equity among such collapsed peoples. Gradually the idea caught on. Progress had to be slow. Benedict could go to no one, as could Francis, begging. He could not white-mail a newly capitalized society. He had to reinvent a subsistence agriculture, republish a practical scholarship and shape into a psychological praxis, for character formation and social cohesion, a liturgy, the elements of which had been written for utterly different purposes and whose liturgical form had been constructed to help solitaries, not to remember their neighbor but to forget themselves.[2]

[2] Yet as Dom. McCann in his book *St. Benedict* points out, St. Benedict himself seems hardly to have realized what he was actually doing; and perhaps he was personally as little responsible for the cultural contribution made by his order as was Gautama for the art of later Buddhism. Benedict wanted his monks taught to read that they might say the office and understand the Scriptures. It would appear that much of the early inspiration to scholarship came from the two foundations of Cassiodorus who endowed these two religious houses and who himself in 540 retired into the one at Vivarium in south Italy. We know from his preface to his *Institutions* that he had the complete idea of the threefold way of avowed intentional living: prayer, subsistence and scholarship, psychology, economics and education because he tells us that he tried to persuade Pope Agapetus to found a Christian university in Rome itself. His houses, however, failed while his ideas were incorporated in Benedictinism.

So successful was he that it is impossible to say what shape Western culture would have taken had it grown up outside this mold. As we have seen, barbarism turned into medievalism. And so true is it that a reviving culture always springs along that border where the republished ideas of antiquity touch the new raw faith of a baptized rough, that scholasticism flowers in the Bologna and Padua of the Lombards, the Paris of the Franks, the Cologne of the Teutons and the Oxford of the Norman Saxons.

But all the while that these impressive results were accruing, a vast, and in the end a tragic, a fatal mistake was being made. If it is a truth too often forgotten that revolutions take place first in the mind, it is not less true that a mental mistake is in the end more gravely damaging than a practical blunder. The Church had succeeded but under an immense misapprehension. Both the secular and the religious were equally deluded.

What that mistake was we shall see more clearly if we return for a moment to the early Church's classification of merit. That listing ran, we recall, virgins, confessors, martyrs. A time had now come when protesting against society is no longer a virtue. A man who dared now set himself up against authority is no longer the seed of the Church. The Church has grown into a mighty tree and he who aspires to start things over again, and to protest, must be crushed. The word "heretic" means one who thinks for himself. The new rating accordingly is, as we should expect, wholly in terms of social value. The Church now has its nobility, the types it holds up for universal admiration. This is the actual series of ranks that one must go through to be "raised to the altar," to

[165]

be canonized: Venerable or worthy; Beatus, blessed; Sanctus, holy, a saint.

Roughly speaking we may say that the worthy, or to use a fine old word lately tarnished, the respectable, are those who fulfill the Law of Justice up to the hilt, in other words, gentlefolk. "Swearing unto their neighbor and disappointing him not, though it be to their own hindrance: not giving their money on usury or swearing so that the innocent might be deceived." Your word is your bond and any avarice is alien to you. Next comes the man who is not only a man of duty but who is happy in doing more than Justice could demand. He fulfills the Law of Equity. The man of duty we praise, but we do not envy him. He is what the eighteenth century called a hard conscientious worker—"a very painful man." But we do envy the man who enjoys doing good. He has emerged from Purgation and has entered Proficiency. Purgation is at best a bore: Proficiency is at the lowest, profoundly interesting. The series is crowned with the man who is holy: hale, whole, complete. The respectable have changed their conduct and we at least reap the benefit: the happy have changed their character and we reap more benefit, but they get more than we. The holy have changed their consciousness and they benefit us more than we know and in ways we hardly suspect. But all their social benefit, incomparable as it is, is only a by-product of their being.

Now these three ranks of men and women are associated with the three great lawful answers to the Five Interrogations. The gentleman is the fine and final flower of Justice. The man who completely fulfills the Law of Equity is the happy man: we sometimes call him a philosopher who actually lives his philosophy or an artist in the supreme art of living. He is not merely scrupulously just in all his deal-

[166]

ings. He is creatively generous in all the five aspects of living: nobly generous in his exercise of power, in use of resources, in the guidance of his family, in the reliance to be put upon his word, in utter freedom from any fear of death. This is the hero. But high as he is, there is above him the third type, as far above him as he is above the basic man who must stick to justice and who, though respectable, is no hero. The saint who fulfills the Law of Love, has entered the Eternal Life now. His is not merely a different character from the average respectable man. He has a different consciousness; he has attained union, perfection.

You may ask at this point where, then, did the Church make its mistake? Precisely here. When monasticism emerged as a social invention, as an invitation and inspiration to the renewal of civilization, the Church had long realized that there were the two classes of men, those who kept the precepts and those who rose to follow the counsels of perfection. But as we have seen, the precepts were lowered to Decalogue level, a level undoubtedly suited to some but not for all who could not aspire to the counsels. The counsels were the Law of Love. Where came in the Law of Equity?

The Church had no official place for this essential middle term. This was to make the mistake of imagining, to quote Wells again, that "the Mind of the Universe can't count above two." The mistake certainly had disastrous results. It damaged man's social evolution in two directions. We have seen one of these. It tried to drive the ordinary man—the man living in the world—down to Decalogue level. It tried, oppositely, to drive the man in the monastery, the brain of the new society, "the religious" up to the level of the Highest Law, a height to

[167]

which only individuals attain. It made no doubt about its mistaken belief. The man in the monastery was declared to be following the Life of Perfection. This he was not doing: he was not fulfilling the Law of Love, but the Law of Equity.

This becomes unmistakably evident when we compare the monastic conventual answer to the Five Interrogations with the Equity answer. They parallel each other in all but one respect. Force is not confined to the height and strength of a lovely example and the weight of reasonable demonstration. Property is not dispensed with but held collectively. The counsel of perfection stressed specifically, "Sell all that thou hast." Monasticism only exchanged the private holding and security of the ordinary layman for a group holding which actually gave greater economic security. In the question of sex alone was the Highest Law attempted, the Law of the Love which sublimates all desire as well as all possessiveness. And here we must note again that the Five Interrogations are five test points in what is a single commandment—to love all mankind as oneself. This is why all moralists have said that to break one commandment is to break all. Deductively we can then say that to give one answer to the Five Questions out of one level of law (in this case the highest level—the Law of Love in regard to sex) and yet only to answer the other four questions at the level of Equity is to make an inconsistent reply and so produce an inconsistent life.

Such was the tragedy of monasticism. Here lies the basic reason for the continual frustrant efforts of men to live group-dedicated lives, a wonderful promise at the start and a disappointment and indeed a scandal at the close. It has been said that the history of monasticism is a story of foundations, corruptions and reforms. The only order which can claim to be "never reformed because never deformed" is the Carthusian; and its success seems to have been due to the fact that it did attempt to recreate the solitary conditions lived by the Egyptian monks and it went further even than they in recession from the world's economy for no Carthusian house ever kept itself by basket weaving.

With the rise of Franciscanism the inconsistency becomes flagrant. To Francis poverty was the essential virtue, the hallmark of perfection. But his life proves that he could not, with all his inspiration, raise men by a mass movement to such a height. He resigned the leadership: the next leader, Brother Elias, was low even by secular standards and was deposed. Before Francis' death, the pope has authorized a rule which contradicts the essentials of Francis' rule. We who are interested even more in the psychology than in the economics of spirituality must view with a sense of tragic significance that it was after these tragic endings of a hope which had seemed materialized in fact, that the infliction of the stigmata was experienced.

The first period of the historical study of the Foundation of the Friars stressed in its own naturalistic optimism the Little Flowers, the bird sermons and the adolescent joy of the troubadour of God. We are now in the second period of a deeper psychological insight which dares face more fully the facts of history. We can see both the fact of failure and of its confession by the man who thought, when he began, that ordinary masses of men could continue out of pure love what had begun in a burst of enthusiasm. It is the later Francis himself (long before Ignatius who is usually credited with the grim remark), who rules that the novice must be "like a corpse in his director's hands." Could any picture be more daunting to those in love with a springtime spontaneity? And the practical legacy of Francis is, as Père Poulain points out, to the extremes of psychophysiology and not to the healthy norms of human economy. Before his time there is no record of the infliction of the stigmata. Ever afterwards in each generation especially in his Order such cases have been recorded. Surely this is a challenging conclusion to a story which began by saying that the way of spontaneous love is the way for all and by it and it alone will mankind be brought quickly and en masse to the solution of all its difficulties by the law's perfect fulfillment in complete love?

Meanwhile Francis' Order and all the orders in succession down to the Jesuits, Salesians, Oratorians, reformed Carmelites, etc. went the double path. The majority of the members and their houses developed, after the first enthusiasm, high intelligence which became subtilized into prevaricatory apologetics. Of these the late Scholastic over-definitions are a perfect example and these led that subtle, conforming but desperately concerned man, Cardinal Newman, to cry, "We are not saved by a smart syllogism." Their endless hairsplittings ended in perfunctory thought and lax practice. The economics which developed as each generation tried to correct the error were increasingly practical. First there is the search for endowments until the state became increasingly suspicious of the monastic mortmain—the accumulation of real estate in the hands of what was, in all respects, an undying organization. Then there are services rendered. Neri actually rules that in his new religious company— the Oratory—the members are to retain their private property. The religious collective in which all were a family of unlimited lifelong liability has become, as far as economics are concerned, a gentlemen's dining club with sleeping accommodation added. It is a holy hotel for members duly elected. There was, of course, always a minority of specific contemplatives who, within such orders or in cells attached to them, attempted to live to the full the Law of Perfection, to answer the Five Questions according to the Law of Love. Neri himself is such a one though he preferred to live by being a dolesman, dependent for his daily minimal supply of food on the charity of two of his cardinal disciples.

We may then conclude this section, this inquiry as to how far the brain of medieval Christianity, the specifically religious life, understood what it was doing. We have seen that it was attempting the higher life of Equity but not the highest life of Love. It thought it was following thus the way of perfection. It did in one respect, in answer to the second question (regarding sex) of the Five Interrogations, try to deny itself any less exalted answer than that of universal love. It did not do so in the other four cases. Hence its witness was equivocal, and its practice did not give the average monk or nun such a release of energy that he or she could achieve total liberation from the self. Not only did the monastic orders despise the secular clergy—the parish priests, etc.—there was nearly always acrimonious competition and emulation between the various orders. Monastic loving-kindness often was confined to one's own house.

Man is not made for comfort: comfort can never be his end. It is at best a sane composure and poise, whereby man may work creatively. Man is made for ecstasy; not for a manic elation, but for that sane updrawing of himself from the sheath of the senses, upon attaining which he has achieved the upright position of the spirit, as

[171]

physiologically millions of years previously he achieved the upright posture of his body. This is the real outstanding of himself with complete detachment and objectivity. It is this that gives Liberation and Enlightenment. The message of the Eternal Gospel is that we are each and all called to undergo this second birth and it is for that travail—a word which means work and journey and birth —that we have been given what Sankara calls the privilege of a human body. The body is the womb of the soul. If we will not advance in athletic travail to ecstasy, then we shall fall back on agony. The one thing we may not and cannot rest in is comfort.

Property though held collectively does not relax the grip of ownership nor reassure the onlooker that the joint owner is free of possessiveness. Force (other than argument and example) I must appeal to if others challenge my joint holding and reject my argument. My word cannot be "Yea" and "Nay," the absolute ingenuousness of him who has no other interest than the information of his questioner, if my other joint owners might be embarrassed by my unguarded frankness and generosity. The common store is not mine to give away, as Brother Juniper found so hard to learn. All that I have is not the world's, but my order's.

And, fifthly, a life so lived with an economic security, a material equipment, an aesthetic display and an intellectual prestige surpassing that possessed by the average layman, such a life too often took away not only any desire to enter on the Eternal Life now but even any wish to look forward to that life when this is concluded. The hatching souls in the vast eggs of the monasteries were (to quote Wells again) too often strangled in their own egg membranes. The monasteries did not know that they had achieved Equity. Hence the average monk spent his time in a dangerous complacency believing that he had conformed with the Rule of Perfection and the exceptional monk spent his time in a dangerous despair believing that he had failed in his vocation because he had not attained Perfection.

How far that complacency could verge on cynicism we know from the classic saying of the great Prelate of Cologne whose bon mot Gibbon has translated with his own searching comment: " 'My vow of obedience has made me a Prince Bishop. My vow of poverty has given me an income of 30,000 crowns.' What his third vow gave the reverend gentleman he does not relate." Neither the complacent nor despairing religious could therefore work at the full development of what had actually been achieved—the status and power of a new social pattern, the way of Equity which was monasticism's real contribution to mankind.

In what that might result we shall ask in our final chapter. Meanwhile we shall trace what actual results this unthought-out, but partly worked out, practice of Equity had in Christianized Europe.

X

The Failure of Christendom

WHILE monasticism was "dreeing its weird," fulfilling its destiny, inventing Equity but believing it was demonstrating love, Western mankind was not standing still. On the contrary, under the inspiration of these efforts of the specifically religious and under the guidance of those called the secular clergy, a very distinctive society had emerged. As was said in Part I, here we shall see precipitating itself that fourfold pattern of society which goes back in our social heredity to Sanskrit origins. In the first part we saw that one of the primal demands that is made by man's mind is for a balance. This happens as soon as the human mind first divides into a detached consciousness that distinguishes clearly objective from subjective, and, secondly, divides again into a fore-consciousness directed on the sensa of the outward world and a subconsciousness concerned with non-sensory data. From that time there will be a spiritual and a material world and man will divide his functions, first as a duet and next as a tandem, between these two worlds. These worlds will soon be served by two offices, that of the *sacerdotium* and that of the *regnum*.

Once again these two main divisions will subdivide: the earliest priest is at the very least astronomer, accountant, artist. The earliest king is at the most minimal, chief craftsman, initiator of all activities as well as judge and speaker and permanent president. Osiris, who seems to be a deified priest-king, has as his principal office the planning, the supplying and the solemn opening of the irrigation canal system on which the early Egyptian economy hinged.

The priestly office, then, itself divides into what we may call pure and applied research. The seer type devotes himself to a longer view, a wider apprehension of relationships than the practical priest can have. Second thoughts are better: second sight is still better. The practical priest applies what he can of these deep findings. Often, like much pure research, such findings make nonsense of common sense and no one is able to see their practical value or even their truth. We must remember that pure insight may sometimes be too pure for application. The good is often the worst enemy of the best but conversely the best is not seldom the worst enemy of the good.

In the medieval pattern we see then (Pope Gregory the Great had finally made it uncontrovertible) that the pure researcher, the seer, the contemplative, is the highest member in the social body. The eye is the incomparable organ of sight. You must also expect nothing of it but seeing. Use it otherwise and it is blinded and you are blind. But it need not always be obeyed, though it must be consulted. Not only is it on rare occasions mistaken but frequently it perceives real things about which the rest of the body can do nothing and may need to do nothing. So the contemplative, the purely religious, requires the secular clergy who may, like the other great sense, the sense of touch, decide whether what is seen is within reach and if so can it be handled effectively. The whole of the thought system and administrative system of the creative phase of the Middle Ages was in the hands of those who

[175]

were in some stage of "clerks orders," in some degree churchmen, men whose loyalty was first to Christendom, and only secondarily to their country. The great kings, however effective as men of will, were really only hands, for they were nearly all actually illiterates.

Gradually stemming out from these two extremes of the *sacerdos* and the *rex*, there grew up priests who were mainly administrative technicians and lay folk who were specifically artists and craftsmen.

Hence when medieval society is fully developed it represents fully the caste system of organic human society, that society which always, when complete, has in it the four levels: of priest, knight, merchant and manual laborer. But it is even more important to note that this fourfold society is a *balanced* society. The three degrees of outward secular physical activity are balanced by the three degrees in the inward spiritual understanding. The knight-errant, the merchant venturer, the craftsman journeyman are balanced by the contemplative, the theologian and the bishop. So while the men of action are extending their explorations, enlarging their traffic and exchanging their skills, the men of thought are, as contemplatives, still extending consciousness; as theologians, interpreting the mystics' findings in rational thought; and, as secular clergy, indicating how these interpretations apply to life, limit excess and sanction a growing order.

The more the thirteenth century is studied the clearer it is that this balance was present consciously or unconsciously in the minds of all its great thinkers. The Church then was not a nervously restrictive body anxious to discourage intellectual advance. All its thinkers ask is that every advance in power should have found for it its corresponding balance in purpose. Every increase in means should have its appropriate extension in meaning, every addition in sense-knowledge should be provided with its adequate balance in spiritual insight.

Hence, in spite of the mistake made in the philosophy —or we should better call it the sociology—of monasticism, in the specifically religious pattern of living, nevertheless, for the time being, an actual balanced social order is effected. In the end it is ruined by the inconsistency—the mistake in definition—made in its psychological unit, the monasteries; the grain trust of medievalism failed to do its work, so the whole Catholic Deal failed. Its failure involved the failure of the whole medieval scheme, and, as we have seen, sent the world back in a constant regression in power of cohesion, in a constant search for consent, in a constant demand for a self-sanctioning unity. The increase in expansive physical powers and means, far from solving this difficulty, have, we see, as a historical fact, only made the recessionalism more desperate. "Union now" is a vain cry until psychological insight giving cohesion is equal to physical power giving expansion.

The actual social balance that medievalism temporarily achieved was Christendom. We may examine that term for a moment. It is a term of chivalry: the seven champions of Christendom is a favorite phrase in medieval tales. Analyzed, the term means the Kingdom of Christ. A churchman would have thought of it as the working out of Augustine's *Civitas Dei*. In actual practice it meant that area in which the fourfold structure of society existed, and, therefore, in which there was not an arrested culture, but one in which there was being constantly undertaken that balanced advance of psychological answers demanded by the increase of continual physical discoveries.

A balanced society was possible because within Christendom physical and psychical knowledge were practically equal. The best minds, such as St. Albert the Great (Aquinas' teacher), can teach theology in modern terms, can write a book on botany, advocate strongly the study of all the physical sciences and close his career by summing up his mystical knowledge in the classic booklet, *De Adherendo Deo*. (The actual authorship of this great tractate is now doubted but it so expressed the spirit of his teaching that it certainly is by someone of his school, probably a pupil.) Roger Bacon saw his physical experiments as part of the knowledge needed by the Church to counter mistaken and diabolic knowledge. He said he was researching so that Christians might have powers to resist Antichrist who was shortly coming. And at the very end of the medieval period the great Cardinal Nicholas of Cusa can both advance physical research and teach the methods of that integral thought needed for contemplation. Civilization and Christianity were practically coterminous: religion and culture one. In the single district where this was not so, where the Mohammedan culture touched the frontiers of the Church, there broke out the desperate reactions called the Crusades.

The Crusades corrupted chivalry much as the monastery's misapprehension of its true nature ruined the religion of the Middle Ages. The conception of chivalry had only two alternatives. In the one case the knight met another knight, there was a "debate of arms," "a trial by battle," a duel, and, equally armed and obeying the same fighting rules, the two exercised themselves ("army" and "exercise" in Latin derive from the same root). Each side abided by the arbitrament of arms. The conquered was spared: only the point at issue went to the conqueror. In the other case the knight met a villain, a churl, a bandit or—as the Teutonic knights and knights of the sword in northeastern Europe—a heathen savage. This creature was below the rules of war: he was vermin, not a hunter's noble quarry. He was also (because either outside civilization or inside but denied practice in arms) not really dangerous. In this respect the knight was a controller of noxious animals. With his skill and equipment he need not use great violence or have to invent new and ungentlemanly weapons. The Crusades upset this balance for three reasons. The knight now met a pagan, a man who denied his creed and to whom, therefore, the Church told him to give no quarter. He might convert the northwestern savage but not the Moslem. Further, this pagan was better armed than the Christian knight. Saladin's army had the Damascus steel beside which the swords and armor of the Crusaders were obviously inferior and, even graver disparity, the Saracens now had the terrible Greek fire and before these flame-throwing weapons even the Norman knights blenched. The third and perhaps gravest confusion was, not in difference of faith and disparity of arms, but in disconcerting similarity. Saladin was a knight, a gentleman, a skilled noble, professional fighter. The Crusader had, therefore, to own that he had met his match in every facet. Here was a rival: outside civilization and yet better equipped; outside the Church yet armed with a crusading creed which produced thinkers, yes, and saints; outside chivalry yet by trial of battle proved a very perfect knight. The shock this discovery inflicted on chivalry, on the second level of Christendom's construction, is evidenced in the horrible tragedy of the Templars. Probably the Knights of the Temple did find in Islam a religion nearer their actual needs, and in their rivals in the field a

more appealing ideal than in the shaven celibate priesthood that sent them out to fortress Christendom with
their bodies. Islam was far more a fighter's creed than
Christianity. Certainly the way the pope permitted Philip
of France to destroy a chivalry sworn to acknowledge no
frontiers save those of Christendom, opened the way to
nationalism's open defiance of Christendom itself and
quickly led to the French kings' being able (as a step in
the direction of international anarchy) to put the pope,
the appointed international arbiter, in their pocket.

The collapse of chivalry, following on the equivocal
position of monasticism, left Christendom gravely weak-
ened. Pure psychological research must always be embarrassed when the production of pure researchers, men who
know how to produce integral thought, is not understood.
The monasteries, not knowing how to produce those conditions, become corrupt. Believing they are living the
highest life but in fact living only the higher life, they
make the worst of both worlds. Frustrated from attaining
the change of consciousness which the highest life can
bestow, they fail to live the life of Equity which they
might have achieved. They do not gain vision but neither
can they give that example of successful co-operative living which, with changed character, living in Equity, they
might have given mankind. Their partner the knight has
gone. The Church has sold out the nucleus of an international police force, or rather a supernational army of a
Christendom coterminous with civilization, to that idea's
most deadly enemy—nationalism.

Hence, though medievalism nearly answered the Five
Interrogations, in the end it failed and the sphinx de-
stroyed the society which could not give the right reply.
The Five Questions might have found themselves an-

swered in the highest category, by the Law of Love, by the contemplatives, the pure researchers in psychological understanding, the men of direct vision. The second category, the answer of Equity, might have been given in each of the five requirements: (1) by the knight answering for Force by chivalry; (2) by the religious house answering for Property by co-operation and teaching this way of living to the merchant who could supply the knight with professionally earned livelihood (3) by Sacramental Sex sanctioning all familial relationships in every class; (4) the knight's word of honor and his vow of chivalry, the religious vow of obedience and chastity could have mediated to the merchant the idea and inspiration that his word must also be his bond and to the craftsman that his guild honor was at stake in the hallmark quality of his goods. Fifthly and finally, a true psychology could have taught all four classes, according to their degree of apprehension the true answer to the question, "What is Thought?" They could each have been made to realize to the degree that they stood in need of that knowledge that Thought is the primary fact, that consciousness is *sui generis*. From this they could each and all be shown that, even by those to whom the present life is still the main good, "death is not to be feared." Thus there could have been an integrated organic society. As it was medievalism failed, it is true. But the offer is still open: Before we close we may then return to this hope.

Here we must note the final efforts made by Christendom to control and balance physical invention which now began to become unstinted, as the religious house was ceasing to press forward in thought and the knight had ceased to be the ideal of the civilized man of action. The energy which had gone into the practice of chivalry now turned to business invention, economic enterprise, mechanical devising. And all this was either solely for profit, or, irresponsibly, just to see what would happen.[1] It could not be otherwise, for the governor in the wheel of mechanical progress had ceased to govern, the balancing progression of psychological discovery had come to a halt.

The steady increase of the physical violence used by the Inquisition may be taken as a criterion of the steady decline in the spiritual power of the specifically religious. For it is a certain sign that free consent to and rational argument for a law is waning, when there is a horrible increase in the penalties with which authority tries to impose obedience on those who feel no wish and see no reason to obey. The collapse is not immediate. Repeated efforts are made by conscientious churchmen to devise such psychological rules as would balance the constant growth of economic inventions. The just price was continually ordered. "Regrating and forestalling," ordinary practices in wholesale capitalistic business, were denounced and frequently punished by death. St. Bernardino of Siena, a strict (observant) Franciscan, is thought by some modern economists to have made real contributions to that science.

But by the close of the fourteenth century the thinkers who rouse most interest are not men attempting to make the *status quo* work. They are, though still in the Church, its critics. A man of great influence, if only because the Hussite movement took its thinking from him, is the English priest, John Wycliffe. His theory of the *Domin-*

[1] The research in atomic physics which now, according to Einstein, can and will destroy "two thirds of the human race" unless we can make the prodigious effort of setting up a world state, was begun and almost completed in this spirit of moral irresponsibility.

ium is important, for in it he is stressing the double principle noted above: viz., that Christianity must be Christendom, an area in which every civil activity has its spiritual complement. The Church and the State are indeed one mystical body, and, that being so, a religious person must be religious, and one who wields spiritual power and claims spiritual insight must be spiritual. Surely there is not anything unreasonable in such propositions? As surely they were very awkward for a Church whose practitioners had, with the acquisition of power, lost their hold on principle, and whose seers were compelled only to see what traditional authority had already ruled was to be seen. Wycliffe ended in open opposition and it is interesting that his bitterest denunciations are against the lives of those very friars who were supposed in particular to demonstrate in their lives the Life of Perfection.

We have now reached the sixth stage in the history of Christendom. The papacy has been for two generations in the power of France, and is only released from that vassalage to split in two during a schism of as nearly as many years. Rates of interest, so long wholly denied as usury, are introduced everywhere where trade is advancing. In war, artillery is making battle increasingly a massacre rather than a duel. The Spartan said at Sphacteria when captured by being smoked into a glen and there given the choice, surrender or be shot down, "The arrow does not choose between a brave man and a coward." In that phrase the refutation and the genetic argument for war, that it is natural selection that works on the battlefield, was written so that he who runs might read. Guns underlined that ruling, bombing planes have ringed it round with red, the atom bomb has put the exclamation mark over

[183]

the period. Will anybody so learn? Men cannot. However deadly the ultimate outcome they will use wrong force if they are not given right. If they are temporarily successful with violence they escape what they believed to have been immediate destruction, and when the wheel comes round and the destruction they caused claims them, they fail to realize the causality. They deny that they created the peril that now faces them and blame others for it.

The Church now rapidly became involved in its own desperate issues and fought only to preserve its organization. It failed, and after a short period when it seemed that Christendom would split into a North and a South, a worse fate befell it and it was shattered into a score of states calling themselves sovereign and each attempting to consume its neighbors.

We can now understand why the decline and collapse of religion sees the rapid increase of physical invention. Not only does the energy which went in prayer and was locked up in ritual now go in business and turn to physical invention and exploration.[2] But also the last controls, now merely inhibitions and no longer balances made by equal psychological insights, have vanished.

Henry VIII of England is a typical monarch of the new absolutism. He makes himself head of the Church and the *regnum* usurps the seat of the *sacerdotium*. The sword tries to sanction itself and Erastianism extinguishes the last ember—the possibilities of vision arising among the clergy. After the Thirty Years' War in Germany a peace of exhaustion is patched on the same principle. The subjects of each state must accept the religion of their ruler. Bossuet a little later can deliver from the pulpit before Louis XIV the amazing statement, "Jesus Christ: the

[2] See R. H. Tawney, *Religion and the Rise of Capitalism.*

[184]

Church: the King—God under these three names." No wonder he was an acceptable court preacher. No wonder religion could put no check in the downward path of that international anarchy wherein everyone exchanged physical powers and none kept promises: where every physical invention was common property and all spiritual powers were regarded as mere superstition and fantastic "Enthusiasm."

With the rise of fully conscious nationalism Christianity might be said to enter a seventh epoch. It can, however, scarcely so be numbered. For in comparison with the six previous epochs this last phase can hardly be called Christian. At its rise Christianity was in a world obsessed with religion, a world which when it opposed the Church did not despise it. During its middle phase Christianity is the religion of Western man. In this seventh phase this religion is first nationalism and then economics, and Christianity is treated as a personal private taste such as art. The congruence of Christianity and culture, the balance of an equally advanced psychology and physics was confessed by Christians to be no longer tenable. It is not a historic accident that where nationalism rises and these sovereign states claim to have no moral overlord, there monasticism is destroyed. We need not defend the actual religious communities of the sixteenth century if we maintain that the disappearance of all organized religious living was a grave loss. Not only did their practice need reform: as we have seen, their theory had in it a grave misapprehension. Nevertheless the attempt they made to live the highest life—the Law of Love—and the degree to which they achieved the higher life—the Law of Equity—both deserve more understanding than they have been granted.

[185]

With the triumph of Protestantism among the northern peoples organized religious living was abolished. Only two social patterns were permissible: the family and the nation. Any legal loyalty to a unit larger than the nation was treason: any domestic grouping larger than the family was treated as unnatural. Such a solution was of its nature lacking any stability. Nationalism is that transitory balance between a rapidly expanding economic area insuring maximum economic returns, and as rapidly shrinking a unit of consent. We must repeat this observation, for it has escaped notice. And until we realize that a civilization which attempts to provide psychological cohesion by physical expansion is a society which must shrink and contract psychically *because* it is expanding physically— we shall remain blind to the cataclysmic dynamics of our present culture.

Christendom gone, the seer dismissed, the knight made subject to a king and not to a supreme moral law, Christianity has been in retreat since the peace of Westphalia three centuries ago. It had ceased to be a policy: with the rise of *laissez faire* it ceased to be an economy. It could only remain as a private therapy, a psychiatry. In our own day we have seen even that last province invaded. The last psychiatric method of changing character—conversion —became discredited. As Dr. Sheldon points out in *The Varieties of Temperament*, the violent conversion is most common among people who are mainly athletic and not critical. Our education is aimed not at making people creative but critical. We attempt to raise still further that barrier between the deep creative mind and the surface critical intelligence. Education, terrified of the damage which skillful but tendentious suggestion does to the un-guarded mind, attempts to make all access to that powerful deep impossible. Not knowing how to make men creative and capable of faith, it aims only at making them incapable of delusion and credulity. The effort is vain. A man must believe something: he must create something: either a deadly illusion or a life-giving vision. The irrelevance of the senses must be brought together into some unity. It is the country from which came the ideal of the specialized Ph.D. which fell for an uncritical and blind belief in a leadership itself as ignorant as it was brutal. And not only has conversion been discredited, an alternative method has taken the field. A college student who would feel that he or she had lost intellectual caste if converted, even if it meant freedom from incipient dipsomania, frequently shows a certain pride if he can say that he has spent a thousand dollars on being psychoanalyzed.

The whole of this pattern has been difficult to detect under the swirl of events. But, under the waves and the backwashes, a tide, we can now see, has been setting. The difficulty of judging the worsening of the international moral climate has been due to a lag, or a series of lags. The mills of God grind slowly and outraged laws sometimes only send in their bills to the children of them that broke them. But understanding law means tracing effect and cause back to their source. Even the Decalogue knows that penalties are exacted to the third and fourth generation. For example, the breakdown of chivalry did not lead to a permanent worsening of war, at once. After the wars of religion, armies regain quite a degree of chivalry in the eighteenth century. This was due to two things. The Church had, owing to its own decrepitude, lost its hold on the soldiers long before the Reformation. Indeed some historians maintain that the highest integration of

[187]

the knight and the priest, the moment when the sword and keys were approaching reciprocant interaction, was when in the eleventh century a pope can call an emperor to heel and the feudal system of loyalty to an overlord does not, at least in theory, stop short at the local king but runs right through and up to the emperor. So late does this idea still linger that an imperial visitor making a landing in Britain in the fifteenth century was met by the king's relations who rode out into the sea to challenge and resist his visit unless he promised before landing that he came with no intention of claiming sovereignty.

Secondly, with the breakdown of Christendom, professional armies, retained for constant war which was endemic in the international anarchy, began to have their own codes. They were kept as gladiators and *condottieri* and, like such, they felt a contempt for those who hired men to kill for them and kinship with their opposite professional number. Only with the Napoleonic Wars, with conscription and the levee en masse did war again become unprofessionalized and resume its descent.

On the other hand, the disappearance of the spiritual pure researcher, the contemplative, was also not felt for some time and for one of the same reasons. As Brémond in *Sentiments Religieuses* has shown, the sixteenth century, the century of the Reformation, was a period of slackness and scandal in the religious houses. Gerard Groote and Gerson show the oncomings of this: John of the Cross and Theresa give scathing comment on the state of things in which scandal they found challenge and impetus to reform. By the seventeenth century there is a religious reform in Catholicism as remarkable as that in Protestantism. Indeed non-Catholics need to reflect whether it is not the Church, which is attacked and seceded from, which

[188]

under the shock of its loss does not learn its lesson as well as, if not better than, the Church which in elation at freedom thought that severance from a corrupt authority was all that was needed to make Christian men able to attain salvation. Perhaps we may see on a small topical scale the same thing taking place today in the aftermath of that too hopeful essay in education which called itself Progressive. The seventeenth century which sees the rise of self-conscious nationalism, first in France, saw a corresponding rise of spirituality. This spirituality cannot, however, reverse the degenerative process. The Roman Church has become too rigid, and, when the Quietist controversy ruins research into spirituality, men's loyalty finds no alternative, equal in power to the appeal of the nation.[3]

The factors that made the Protestant world for a while unaware of its loss, were: (1) increase in material prosperity among the well-to-do (the poor, however, were poorer during the eighteenth century, as Thorold Roger points out in his book, *Wages in Britain*); (2) a belief that Reason would demonstrate to men how it was sensible and beneficial to live and they then would so live. The study of rational law in the physical world was giving increasing control over outer nature. Therefore the study and application of rational law in human conduct must give an equal and equally extending control over the psychical world, over human nature. When that faith failed with Hume's skepticism and his demonstration that "There is no *reason* why I should prefer the pricking of my finger to the death of a hundred human beings," then the dynamic genius of a Wesley takes refuge in emphasizing human depravity and showing that by a convulsive experience of the self's bankruptcy and God's free Grace

[3] See Saudreau, *Life of Union with God.*

[189]

the individual's character can be changed. So the skeptical philosophy and the practical creative religion of the day both told against any science of the soul and any persistent research into the growth in grace, the evolution of consciousness. One solitary figure in Protestantism seems to have carried on this research, but even he failed to make practical applications of it. William Law, after becoming a famous controversialist and writing in his *Serious Call* one of the best sellers religion has produced, realized that conversion and amendment of life were not enough. It was Jacob Boehme's strange but authentic writings that put this master of quiet style and seemly manners, as he says, "into a sweat" as he read in those darkly luminous passages real tidings of what the soul could become and was called to become: the revelation of the Eternal Gospel summoning man to his real vocation, his second birth, that emergence into a change not merely of character but of consciousness, into a state of completion, wholeness, union, holiness, as much above goodness as goodness is above evil. Wesley, however, attacked Law for making the path to holiness too exacting. Further, Law himself apparently saw this only as a personal quest, a private individual exploration. He seems to have thought of the highest spirituality more as a mountain peak to which an explorer goes, rather than a scientific secret which in a laboratory a pure researcher strives all his life to unravel in order that a new discovery and invention may be given to mankind, an invention which can and alone can balance man's increasingly unbalanced powers in the physical world.

Certainly it is that after Law no Protestant explorer went so far, still less brought back discoveries. Again, the increasingly dangerous lack of advance was shrouded from men by activity. Missions revived and men who knew the

[190]

Alpha of the Gospel rushed out to teach the whole to others of different creeds. They destroyed more than they understood, and though their enthusiasm and self-sacrifice is beyond praise and their individual triumphs with individual souls redound to God's glory, they had at best only a psychiatry, an answer to man's individual psychological problem, his sense of personal guilt, and not an answer also to his economy and his policy. Their results, therefore, were not only limited but in part actually harmful.

It is vital that this point should be stressed. It is the "fortified line" of the resistance to the real religious revival. Bitter jests, such as, "When Britain says the Gospel she means Cotton," may be disregarded. But when such capable and widely informed authors, economists and sociologists as F. A. Hayek (*The Road to Serfdom*), K. Polanyi (*The Great Transformation*) and P. F. Drucker (*The End of Economic Man*), all agree that the economic phase is over and that man, if he is to survive, must find a psychosocial sanction, their criticisms of religion are not hostile and must be met. Polanyi and Drucker feel that the churches are not proving adequate to their critical opportunity because they have not a sociology. They can give mankind no goal of development to take the place of the economic utopianism which has proved to be delusory. A return to the past has been proved impossible, through the failure of totalitarianism. Such books as Professor William Macneile Dixon's *Human Situation* have proved that the dream of raising everyone to a level of economic and physical permanent prosperity is equally vain. The third alternative, the evolution of consciousness and the development of man through growth of the spirit, the churches have neglected, and are ignorant of the fact

[191]

that this psychiatry can and does inevitably lead to an appropriate economy and policy. To begin with the spirit of man is not escapism but realism: to stop with the solution of the individual's conflict is to begin to act with a still unfinished diagnosis. Man's individual psychosis and neurosis are part of his social dislocation. The healing of the individual depends on creating that environment in which a healthy individual soul can subsist. Conversely a healthy society depends on its units, sane individuals. There is no conflict between the good of the individual and that of the group—they are complementary. It is the discovery of that fact which makes anthropology the science that today is about to succeed to the throne left vacant by the abdication of economics. As Polanyi points out, the epoch of thinking which broke out with Adam Smith's crystallization of the idea of economic man, that man's chief motive power is his wish for material gain, is closing. Its place is being taken by the anthropological concept of values—that man seeks approval more than gain. Missionary effort, based then on, at best, an individualistic psychiatry and lacking a real social gospel, an economy equal to its psychology, a sociology to balance its eschatology, only opened the door to the economic exploitation of its converts. "Trade follows the flag" was a none too reassuring slogan of "the nation of shopkeepers" when told to "think imperially." Further observation added a prior term to the flag. The flag follows the cross. As an actual and tragic fact and because the modern Christian propaganda had no economy or policy, in the wake of salvation followed exploitation and "the reproach of the gospel" took on another and more terrible meaning than Paul ever intended or imagined.

In the Roman Church, too, a magnificent missionary

[192]

effort to bring comfort to individual souls, spread over the world. The Jesuits not wholly undeserving the blame that even a pope put upon them for their political activities in Europe, in almost every other quarter of the globe —from Paraguay to Canada—from Africa to Japan— showed a devoted and skilled heroism which may be equalled but can hardly be surpassed. But though personally marvelously kind to slaves and all sufferers, save heretics, they did not protest against the horror of the slave trade nor any of the imperialisms of the political powers who permitted them to proselytize. As we have seen, actual research in advanced spirituality had in Catholicism been arrested by the end of the seventeenth century, with the Quietist controversy. The Jesuits themselves, tied to the Ignatian exercises, had largely spurred on this repression. The penalty was inevitable. By the close of the seventeenth century and through the succeeding generations, intense spirituality of commanding power can only be produced by men and women of poor critical intelligence. This poor intelligence confines their witness to those of their exclusive communion. It makes them approve doctrines not permissible to a thinking charity such as Eternal damnation, and keeps them—through subservient loyalty of the absolute obedience required by that Church—from obeying the dictates of a larger charity, which their actual direct experience of God would instill, and also from working out any of those economic and political conclusions to which the vision of the Eternal Gospel points.

Such, then, I would venture to present to you as a tentative outline of Christianity's contribution or emphasis to and in the Eternal Gospel. I would repeat that though social reform has been great and though Christian-

[193]

ity has in Protestantism in the last few generations associated itself with that effort, such reform and such association are not adequate. Not only are tares and wheat growing together: surely none can doubt that the tares are gaining on the wheat? The problem, if we look at it frankly, is so serious because in its acutest form—that of the international anarchy—the greatest danger lies not so much from evil men but from huge and increasing physical powers which we cannot control and which good men feel they must use and do use to impose their ideas of right. Not only is war today increasingly violent and so creating increasing shock on those who use it and on whom it is used. Not only do nations take longer now to recover from the resentments which such methods arouse. Not only will any average man hate a foe who has burned alive his children, but the man who burns alive another's children has to believe his victim to be forever outside humanity's pale. An even worse danger is the immense and ever-increasing unprecision of modern warfare. It destroys millions who had no part in the original *casus belli*.

The Church may be doing and may do a considerable amount to raise the economic standard of a country which has food surpluses, by white-mailing big business to be more generous with its surplus. But this is merely a meliorative process and depends, if it is to continue, on two things. The first may be true: it may be possible to increase the yield per acre far beyond present limits, but in the end Malthus' "devil" must appear at the board. The only answer to him is birth control and we must remember that what is still in all probability the strongest Church and certainly the one which finds it hardest to rescind a decision, has decided against such inventions.

[194]

Here is one more example, as with the rise of money, of our psychological progress not being able to keep up with physical progress. The second is certainly not true: that where the standard of life rises, there men become more peaceful, wiser, more self-controlled. In international affairs, where the armament competition may compel a nation, concerned to raise its own standard, to have to lower it to meet the risk of aggression, in that world, where the tempo of civilization and indeed its course is set by the most brutal bidder, religion has never been more demonstrably helpless. The demand today is not for new ends or lofty goals: it is for means, for a quality of power able to deal with the powers which aggressors can employ, and yet of such a quality that the power will not, as does present military power, frustrate the aims of idealists. Nor, as we have seen, is religion any more successful at the other endangered sector of society: the internal front. There, too, the problems of criminality and lunacy do not call for an increase of economic resources or more coercive force; they call for a power which can effect the twisted and inturned consciousness of that huge and increasing population which defies order and drains courage and good will.

The problem of religion today is then a question of research. Can we rebalance our knowledge, can we find spiritual powers equal to our unbalanced physical powers? This research is for no private satisfaction. It is no more escapist and asocial than is research into atomic physics. Indeed it can claim to be far less so. In each case the pure researcher must find and abide by those conditions which govern his research. To deny these, to demand that pure research be immediately practical, is not to show oneself a business man but a barbarian. The finding of this power

[195]

is a matter of life and death for civilization itself. By God's mercy we know that it can be found and we know also that it and it alone solves our almost desperate problem. But the price is, we need hardly say, high. It is the Pearl of Great Price and for that a man must give all that he has.

May I then give the concluding part of these lectures to a projection: Therein I will try to show from the point where Christianity finds itself today, along what path it might go to commend the Eternal Gospel to mankind and, through it, hope to fulfill the promise that it does bring peace to men of good will.

PART III

Prognosis

XI

The Doctrine of Redemption and Technics of Training

SUCH, then, has been the Christian effort to implement and actualize the Eternal Gospel. The appeal today is pragmatic. Men ask, not, What does a religion preach? but, How does it practice? We are told to remember that the proof of the pudding is not in the cookbook but in the eating. It is history that is to decide whether a religion is true, for the verb "to be true" has become synonymous with the verb "to work." We may, and I believe we should, allow all this as a truth and one that has been neglected. It is a form of that efficient instrument, the Razor of William of Occam, brought out and given some necessary cutting to do.

But, at the same time, we should not forget to note that it is not the only truth. No philosophy is completely explicated and expressed by its practices and therefore no philosophy can be wholly disproved by its practitioners. Applied research never employs the whole of pure research and, for that reason alone, the mistakes of those who apply the findings of pure research can never wholly discredit or disprove that research.

The Eternal Gospel is more than the highest achievements of human sanctity and Christianity is more than the entire history of the Christian Church. Cardinal Bérulle, the seventeenth century saint, uncanonized as yet but called by his contemporary pope when he made him cardinal, "Apostle of the Incarnate Word," nevertheless always kept with a special veneration the Feasts of All Souls and All Saints. For, he said, that until the last soul that shall attain sanctification has lived and died the blessed Mystery of the Incarnation will not be consummated.

May we, then, see first, what were the particular emphases that Christian theology stressed in the Everlasting Gospel and next glance, in conclusion, at the specific psychological practices whereby Christian practice strove to make those elements of the Gospel work in men's lives. From these considerations we may gain a foresight into the future of religion and, as the whole of this thesis turns upon the supreme need of contemporary religion for contemporary man, we may perhaps gain some concept of the direction in which mankind must go if it would survive and progress.

As we saw at the start, though, in the Eternal Gospel, the Trinitarian concept is present in a number of the later interpretations, in Christianity the emphasis is not merely Trinitarian but, in the interpretation of the Persons as aspects of the Godhead's nature in relation to man, the Second Person is that aspect under which the soul is considered first to know God. That aspect is one of Redemption. Vishnu also is the sustainer and restorer of the universe which Brahma creates. He is therefore naturally that aspect from which the avatars, the incarnations of God who lead men back to Deity, emerge. But the difference of what is meant by Redemption in the East and the West is shown with startling vividness when we compare the figures of the Johannine Jesus and even the Krishna of the Bhagavad-Gita. Redemptive Love as understood in the West may often be misrepresented by its terminology. It can certainly

[200]

be made ridiculous and even repulsive when certain statements about blood are used by apologists to commend and by critics to discredit what neither wish to understand. The issue, however, has been put clearly and fairly—by that I mean in arguable terms—by Bernard Shaw when he makes the case against Redemption by saying that each man has to discharge his own debts.

Now we have seen that though such a case might be argued formerly, the argument will not hold today. It is prepsychological and pre-anthropological. As a fact of observation we are not individuals. Our social heredity has made us very largely what we are.[1] Paul was nearer the anthropological truth when he said, "No man liveth unto himself and no man dieth unto himself." The Christian doctrine of Forgiveness and Redemption is based on the principle that if the higher can go to the lower, he can as it were give a transfusion of help—the doctrine of Grace—and by this help the lower can rise. Salvation is this act of good will whereby that which has, comes down to the level of that which has not. All that is asked of the one in need is that he shall be willing to accept. That act of the will permits Grace to enter. Nor is this act one of easy condescension, a kind of patronizing pity which, with almost a streak of contempt, lifts a debased creature out of the mire. The doctrine of Redemption is not a contravention of Law. All it states is that if you can recognize solidarity and unlimited liability then you will be able to see that there is no one so low but you are part of him and your compassion may raise him.

Two things are required and they are both law-ful: The first is that you should recognize your "kinship" with the low, you should have real love for him (and not treat him

[1] See J. A. Singh and R. M. Zingg, *Wolf Children and Feral Man.*

simply as a social nuisance to be salvaged like a dead whale). The second is that, recognizing that kinship, you should own that you actually did what he did. This admission goes even further than the lofty doctrine of the Bodhisattva in Mahayana Buddhism. The fine side of that doctrine is that it mobilizes each soul arriving at Salvation for permanent service to the end of time for every creature that can be conscious of suffering. The fine side of Christianity is that it bends to the very level of the enslaved soul in order to set it free. It maintains that by so accepting and understanding why the weak failed, the strong can, and they alone, so become one with the failure, that the strength of the strong may flow into the weak and they may rise. A religion so lofty and so deep in its understanding of human solidarity only needs to rid itself of the inconsistency of Private Salvation to become one of universal appeal. The doctrine of Private Salvation owes so much to that narrow cosmology which the subapostolic age took from Jewish Apocalypse that with the change in cosmology may we not hope that this narrowing of the Eternal Gospel, which proves such a barrier to the spread of the Good News, may be removed by those who have the courage of love?

This is not, of course, to preach an emasculated gospel. Indeed we may say that if we follow actual experience we shall see that though loans may be granted to those who would again set about the business of Salvation they are, to the end of time, loans. The law must be kept and, as said earlier, because the judge pays the fine, if the debtor would really become as free as the judge, when he is given his loaned freedom the first thing he must do is to discharge the debt, from the paralyzing pressure of which the judge has temporarily relieved him. Here the Law of Equity, in its treatment of bankruptcy, can help us to work out the Law of Love in regard to moral bankruptcy. I would suggest that the Eternal Gospel was only making its outlines more clear when the Christian Church, aware that apocalypticism had become irrelevant and that, therefore, throughout the centuries millions of souls would leave this life in conditions of rudimentary salvation, began to teach with Irenaeus and defined with Gregory the doctrine that after death men may pay and must pay for what is uncompleted in this life. Irrevocability may indeed enter when we pass from time into Eternity. But there is no evidence that physical death ends the temporal experience for the individual soul and as God is the Eternal there seems good reason that, when Eternity is attained, union with Him must take place. God cannot have an eternal rival else He would have created an evil equal in power to Himself. God gives to man every gift save the gift of Eternity—otherwise man could do permanent damage to himself and maybe to others.

This doctrine of Eternity and Salvation brings in the second emphasis: Beside Redemption as a power which actually accepts the sinner's failure as its own, there is in Christianity a strongly stressed doctrine of Sanctification. It is true that when the doctrine of Redemption is degraded, to bargain or magic, from its station as the highest manifestation of love, then the doctrine of Sanctification, which is its complement, suffers an eclipse. The Holy Ghost ceases to be a loved and constantly helpful concept of God wherever the doctrine of a blood sacrifice makes Salvation no more than a method of escaping the wrath of God.

As was said at the beginning of this essay, the doctrine of Sanctification envisages two things. In the first place, it looks forward to the soul not merely being salvaged but to

[203]

its growing in grace and in knowledge. Salvation is begun by Redemption but only completed by Sanctification. The second implication is that the temporal experience is not simply a mistake but that the soul which is recreated by Redemption can now proceed upward and become something greater and more valuable than it would have been had it remained simply without stain but without effort.

Here we are on the threshold of the vastest of metaphysical problems: Why God created the world—the problem which contains in itself the seed of all the theological problems. Today they are neglected because when men saw that a logically watertight system could not be devised they mainly lost interest in pure theology as an unhelpful form of speculation. If we remember, however, that theology is a working science we shall recognize it to be something in the nature of an extrapolated psychology and epistemology. Theology should not then be afraid of antinomies, for an antinomy is the result of binocular vision which has yet to attain bifocal balance. Theology's task is to reconcile the findings of the analytic intelligence, which expresses itself in logic, with the apprehensions of the integral intelligence which operates by insight. If we agree that the phenomenal world is a construction, and not an illusion, then we must allow that our normal experiences of it, though partial and sometimes distorted, can be seen to supplement and not to contradict the seer's knowledge of the noumenal universe.

I am offering in an Appendix three suggestions as to a possible present-day statement on three problems of experience to which the old orthodoxy gave explanations under the terms Original Sin, Salvation and Eternal Damnation. These explanations the world has now rejected, though it has not solved the problems themselves which give rise to the explanations.

In concluding this main essay I would venture to indicate at this point the praxis whereby Christianity strove to give a method which would help men to express and sustain in their lives the truths which it emphasized. First among these methods is Sacramentalism. This subject is one more of those which, seeming to be closed, has again opened. The prepsychological age of anthropology, which had its summing up in Frazer's *Golden Bough*, thought that with its explanation of Totemism it had dismissed Sacramentalism—at least in that Eucharistic form which Christianity developed. But now that Totemism itself is being found to be a mysterious matter—much more mysterious than they imagined who had not troubled to win the confidence of those who practiced it—Sacramentalism, too, must be re-examined. It would seem that the identification which man may extend so that he enlarges his sense of being in order to embrace his fellows, need not stop short with humanity. Indeed if that identification is to bring to man not only union with himself and with his fellows, but with all life, then of necessity he must be able to realize that common life flowing in all its living forms. He may then attain to a sense of kinship which is without that anthropomorphic sentimentality which would think of animals as manikins or that mechanistic contempt which would regard them as machines. Moreover, with such a standpoint, man dare face the facts of death, symbiosis and mutual sacrifice. For he recognizes under the changing forms not merely different qualities of consciousness—and so the problem of suffering is seen from a deeper standpoint—but he realizes that the persona is not the thing of essential value. That essential value is the Eternal Life running through all, the flame inextinguishable which takes the shape of the jet through which it blows, but when the jet is broken, is itself free to manifest elsewhere.

The development of Sacramentalism in the Church was very definite. As Loisy has pointed out, there was first the Eucharist of the Saviour God and this was followed by what he has called the Eucharist of the Paraclete. In the first part there was the experience of Redemption and Redemptive Love. In the second there was the experience of the charismata. The first was restorative of a broken unity. The second was the continuation of a creation which sin had interrupted. This issue should be of particular interest to Baptists. For the sacrament of Water and Fire—in distinction from the sacrament of Blood and Wine—is essentially the Eucharist of the Holy Ghost. One would venture to ask, May it not be that here we discover a reason why the Church has been backward in extending the knowledge of the charismata and has stressed Salvation to the considerable neglect of Sanctification? While the Eucharist of Salvation—the Mass—was developed into the central rite of repeated restoration, Baptism was made an initial rite and, save among the Baptists, reduced almost to a rudimentary procedure in which the person—the infant—could take no conscious part. This made the process one which could easily relapse into superstition and, in any case, would have little to do with its early association with the Paraclete and His Gifts.

It is worth repeating in this context that Nicholas Berdyaev has pointed out that in the Greek Orthodox Church the Great Desolation of the mystics' experience in the West, is not found, and that he attributes to the Third Person being more worshiped in the East than in the West. It would seem that when Salvation remains the final term of a man's spiritual experience, and when he does not

[206]

proceed to Sanctification, he will have no experience of that change of consciousness, that *metanoia*, out of which there springs the charismata. He will be still a "backward looking man," and, therefore, as his sense of God's greatness increases, he will still be comparing That with the fallen self he was. He does hate sin, but, as he has no deep experience of a complete change of consciousness, he will often —as do many proficients of this stage and this cultus— suffer acutely from doubts as to whether he really has been saved, and the thought of meeting his Maker, whether after this life for the non-mystic or in this life for the mystic— will be fraught with terror.

That the double sacrament of the Saviour and the Paraclete was meant to conclude with the emergence of the new consciousness, the new life which can say *Vivo jam non ego,* we cannot doubt from the place, the key place, that the word *metanoia* holds in the pristine Church. Our word of translation, "conversion," we all now agree, gives once again evidence of a narrowed interest in Salvation and a neglect of interest in Sanctification. One of the most interesting documents of that period is that church calendar found lately near Alexandria in which it is noted that there are meetings three times a week for *metanoia*. Not even the most charitable of churches could have fought against the discouragement that would arise if three times a week the main part of the congregation needed to be saved all over again. The strict Greek sense of the term can alone explain this entry, and the realization that there was felt the need for constant joint growth in sanctity, in the sense of the common Eternal Life with one another, interprets for us the early Church's praxis. There is, of course, no *conflict* between Salvation and Sanctification any more than the Two Persons of the Trinity are two separate bodies. Sanctification is the necessary extension of Salvation. The tragedy of conversionism lies, of course, precisely here. The issue on this point is not whether conversion is a wise method. That, as we have seen, depends on the type of temperament with which you are dealing. What Dr. Sheldon calls the somatatonic—the man of bodily action—probably always has something of a shock when he realizes that his body is not the final term and that there are immaterial forces about him far stronger than his thews. These truths do not so shock what Sheldon calls the cerebrotonic, and so his conversion is more gradual or at least lacks a shock element in it. What is true of both types and all types is that they all have to persist, whether they start gradually or catastrophically. One is reminded of Bishop Westcott's gentle reply to the Salvation Army lassie who buttonholed him on the top of a London bus with the challenge, "Are you saved?" "In process of being saved, yes, thank God. Saved for good? Ah?"

The development of the praxis in the early Church, whereby men might have true experience of the Eternal Life now, is a fascinating but still very obscure subject. We can only point to a few strange landmarks and I can only ask a few questions and make request that further investigation be undertaken. As the group enthusiasm began to become more formalized and more repressed—for it obviously often required both, as we can have no doubt from Paul's Corinthian letters—the powers tended to be present in a few or one man—though the group undoubtedly helped him to release them. The place of the prophet in the early Church is of the greatest interest, and as Dr. Streeter has said in his book, *The Four Gospels*, the problem of the Fourth Gospel will never be adequately handled until we understand the powers and position of this personage. We can, I believe, get light on this subject if we study those Quaker journals which give descriptions of the traveling adviser who used to visit families and meetings with a message and who, in a state often of what we should call trance, spoke with uncanny insight to the needs of particular persons, needs which sometimes they had hidden from all their friends. It is of value to notice that a church in its early days, such as the Quaker communion, did produce that type which had so much influence in the formative years of the church. The whole matter of healing, of extra-sensory perception and other paranormal capacities is now undergoing a revolutionary revaluation. We are entering on an age as far removed from the narrow rationalism of the Deists as that was from the narrow obscurantism of the late medieval schoolmen. I would venture to beg, as this issue lies so close to the problems of the Church, that those who are responsible for teaching, preaching and counseling should study the difficult but inescapable problems of psychical research. These issues are specifically belonging to theology; these issues, if the Church neglects them, will not go out from men's minds. A critical evaluation of this material does not mean that it should be accepted. What I would venture to maintain is that no one who has studied the subject carefully, say for six months, can fail to come at least to this conclusion: That here is something not only of great importance, not only ill represented by those, in the main, who profess interest in it now but one which belongs to the authorities of spirituality. They and they alone can fit it into a proper frame of reference. Meanwhile, organized research to its honor is now attempting this problem. The co-operation of religion with this exploration will be for the benefit of both science and religion.[2]

[2] See G. W. N. Tyrrell, *Science and Psychical Research.*

The Shepherd of Hermas leaves us in no doubt that the "prophet" marks a rank in the spiritual authorities of the Church, a historical stage which lies between the apostles and the rise of an organized episcopacy. But even should the Church have been able to remain friendly to those who wished to utter truths which they felt both new and inspired, it is doubtful whether this kind of seership would have continued. No doubt dogma and ritual, when they were set, resisted any innovation. But, further, the power of the seer seemed on the decline. The whole subject of the *subintroductae* presents a problem in psychology and indeed in psychophysiology, far too subtle to be handled without a knowledge of endocrinology which such experimental texts such as the Tantric formulae alone seem to offer.[3] We, as historical onlookers, can and must notice two points: First, that the power of conviction is failing in these prophets—they have now to work through a sibyl, a medium; second, that the Church could hardly continue to sanction such procedure—though, when Cyprian condemned the practice, he did not bring charges of looseness against the prophets, but says only, what is undeniable, that the procedure was open to grave misunderstanding on the part of the pagan world.

Increasingly those who wished to find the direct approach to God and a present sense of His Being, were seeking it in the sacraments, especially in the Mass. It is important to note the steady decline of the Agape, the disappearance, save as a funeral feast, of this common meal. The Eucharist itself becomes a rite increasingly stylized and, though witnessed by the people, hardly in fact *coram populo*, but a process performed by a few specialists at the altar. Indeed as that well-known liturgiologist, Canon Dearmer said, in

[3] See Sir John Woodroffe, *Shakta and Shakti*.

Low Mass we see the final decline of a rite once public and communal into the most private of procedures. The group field is no longer being employed and lay folk are in growing danger of their religion being something done for them.

Seership is henceforth increasingly confined to the monasteries. Though the interest in mysticism is today a couple of generations old, it is still hard for Protestant scholars to have any certainty as to the methods actually used in the contemplative orders to attain to full *metanoia*. What we do know is that great insight may be so obtained by such experts. For example, as a valuable light upon the difficult question of guidance, we know—it is just one example of many—that when that remarkable master of prayer, Philip Neri, wishes to know whether he should go as a missionary to India, on such a point he neither trusts his own considerable spiritual insight nor trusts his confessor nor any "religious" in the "world." He has resort—and it is taken for granted he will—to a contemplative monk, a Carthusian, who is known to have attained the power of such guidance. This man says he will seek God's Will for a week; but on Neri's returning for the opinion he is told that God has not given the seeker any light. He is, however, advised, by this truthful guide who has the courage to say he does not know, to consult another contemplative. Here, too, there can be no haste or snap judgment. Another week has to be spent while the second expert seeks as to whether God will reveal His Will to him. Then at last the guidance is found.[4] This is a very different and far more expert picture of guidance than we have been used to being given nowadays. One has a feeling that these earlier masters of prayer knew what they were doing and knew how to dis-

[4] See Capecelatro, *Life of St. Philip Neri*.

tinguish between a true illumination and a private fancy in a way that those who spend little time in prayer in comparison with the time spent on publicity, can hardly hope to emulate.

The two problems, therefore, which confront religion today and for an answer to which the world is asking with a new desperate concern are precisely Guidance, the real gift of insight into God's Will, and Apt Force, the power to use a force which does not frustrate itself. The problem is, of course, one, for these two questions stem from one need: a sanction for society. He who could really foresee, really indicate how law, moral law will work itself out, he would already have much of that apt power which, if society is to be saved, must take the place of that inept violence which is all we have to use to sanction order and peace. It is enough to note what huge sums are now spent in the effort to forecast events to see the value which the present world has to put on even the vaguest indication of what the future may bring forth. The Eternal Gospel has always promised that the single-hearted shall see God, that if the eye be single the body shall be full of light. Certainly, Christianity has not underrated the price that man must pay if he is to win vision. We are blind because we will not clear the eye of the soul from the scar tissue which makes seeing impossible. As long as we are blind we are unable to find our way to lead others. Once we have sight we not only can direct; our vision shows us how we may have whatever increase in apt force, in absolute authenticity, in spiritual power that is needed really to sanction peace and order. One must say, as the writer to the Hebrews concludes his catalogue of the triumphs of Faith, "time would fail to tell" of what that power can do when it is really pure.

We have dismissed these records, as the defeated disciples dismissed the first report of the resurrection, as idle tales, because we do not want to believe. And indeed with good reason, for if this thing is true then it alone can save us. But if it is true then it calls for a permanent mobilization from which most people would gladly be excused. True *metanoia* and its history have an unpleasant analogue with transmutation. For ages men claimed alchemy, for centuries they were proved frauds. Finally it was said authoritatively, transmutation has never been done and never will be. Yet we have lived to see alchemy become part of accepted physics and atomic power released by transmutation. For ages men claimed that it was possible to bring about the alchemy of the soul—*metanoia*—the change of character and of consciousness, and to release the powers so locked up in the ego. Research has certainly been able to lay bare much fraud, to show that the claimed changes were pretenses and even when an apparent alteration of consciousness or character had taken place, it did not endure; there was a relapse into the old pattern and a loss of the new power. During the last century the slogan began to be current, human nature never changes. Psychoanalysis seemed to set the seal on the popular belief, or, should one say, complacent despair. Now, however, no researcher in history or in comparative religions can doubt that the transmutation of the soul, the direct hit on the nucleus, the release of the power of the soul strangulated in the ego, has taken place and does take place. But when we complete the analogy we see how serious is this discovery. As no molecular action, no heat or fire can alter the atom, so no ordinary warmth of good will or enthusiasm for social service will really touch the heart of the trouble, the deep of the ego, the basic clutch and cramp of the self.

[213]

To get to the nucleus of the atom, to hit it and break it there is needed an immense electric charge, one which is far beyond any such charge as men could generate even a couple of generations ago, a charge very dangerous if not carefully handled. If the soul is to be transmuted, a charge of spiritual force as high, and as dangerous if lightly handled, is required. We are not getting these results in the spiritual realm. Why? Because, though in physics, as we now know, there is no risk that we would not take to get the forces that we desire, we shun in religion anything that might even disturb our comfort or take any considerable portion of our time. We hear a great deal from sensible and worldly-successful religious people about the fully-rounded life. We have to ask, Is a fully-rounded life compatible with one that is one-pointed, singlehearted? Has any great triumph of research or exploration, of discovery or invention ever been made by those who did not give their whole attention, their whole lives to the venture? To become a thing with a head, a spine and a drive, the jellyfish had to cease to be fully rounded.

We must then give ourselves to this research which alone can right our capsizing civilization. Man has transmuted the atom—at what cost to the individual and to society we still can hardly guess. But one thing is certain—he must now transmute himself. What was urgent has now become desperate. No assertion that the process is costly, inconvenient, tiring, can be allowed to stand in the way. The other side has been prepared to pay and having paid has been given what it asked—power. The religious side must be prepared to pay, and if it will pay it will be given what it needs—and the world is dying for—vision. So then, though the old pattern of the monastic contemplative may be closed to us, we must see whether the insight and the

[214]

power which came from such traditional methods may not be produced under modern conditions and with modern methods.

First and foremost we require research, experimental research into Prayer. Such minimum requests as must be made in this matter I have put forward in an essay called *A Preface to Prayer,* so I will not repeat them here. Professor Douglas Steere in his *On Beginning from Within* has made two specific demands: (1) for a book of graded methods for spiritual exercises, something that might take the place and fulfill the mission that once the Ignatian Exercises had served; (2) for a new kind of Tertiary Order —a communion of dedicated men and women of prayer, living by their rule of life in the world but not of it. Such an Order would be a living demonstration of the Law of Equity functioning in full and complete practice. From the way of life which this Law would allow these its practitioners to follow there might arise those individual geniuses of religion, those pioneers and leaders of mankind, the saints who practice the Law of Love.

But how could this thing begin, what is the first step? Such a nuclear organism would, one presumes, start as a church. As now has happened in the practice of medicine, a specifically contemporary church today must be a matter of a team and teamwork. There should be in each such nuclear church a central staff of five, each with a special function. Preaching is only one, and a very special, gift of the spirit. Next there should be the director of souls. A great diagnostician is seldom a fine lecturer—the gifts are widely different. The master diagnostician must also be something of a pure researcher. He is always learning more than he can teach, more than he can at the moment apply, seeing into fresh mysteries beyond his power to explain.

[215]

He (and indeed his four colleagues) must regularly go "into Retreat," or, as I feel it is more accurately phrased, on to those advanced posts of foresight-insight. There they gain two things: First, they recover and confirm their long vision—always a little shortened and made myopic by concentration on the immediate and the palliative. Shortened views nearly always mean shortened patience and loss of peace. Secondly, and even more important, there they may learn of new research findings. For always back of them (or rather in advance of them) they must have those pure researchers with whom they have periodic consultation and who are as necessary to advance in creative spirituality as such researchers are to all the advances in applied physics. A third expert is needed to co-ordinate the whole of worship, so that the appeal of religion to those who attend the church, the teaching of it to them and their practice of it may have an integrated consistency. This is far more than merely practicing the art of proper presentation—useful and necessary as that function assuredly is. It is inquiring into and experimenting with the important and almost neglected problem of group psychology as a practical issue of worship and congregational unity. For that we need the study—and the applications of the findings—of the relationships of numbers and quality, of intensity and mass. Does the sense of union, the devotion to the beloved community, grow quickly when there are many? What is the optimum number for worship, for communion, for various forms of associative rite? All these anthropological and sociological questions are arising owing to the increasing study of the "field," which in physics, biology and individual psychology (Gestalt) is becoming of increasing importance and tending to show that the individualistic or atomistic approach was partial and needed this supplement.

Human ecology is becoming a popular and important word. A religious congregation is certainly a unit in which that ecology needs to be studied and would yield valuable results. A number of highly significant anthropological and group-religion facts are now known and their application is obvious, though still neglected. I can only cite as examples two or three: The minimum number of ten which is preserved as the basic unit of association in Jewish worship; the unit of twelve in the Fertility Religions; and the Quaker experience that above twenty there may be a marked sense of loss of the sense of unification, present in the smaller silent meeting.[5] A fourth brother of such a group should have as his care, not preaching or individual counseling but the taking of those graded classes, so that people may really be educated in the religious life, knowing its stages and learning to equip themselves to function in increasingly expert grades. The fifth, one imagines, would serve this small collegium by being its liaison officer and keeping touch with the other churches, finding out those with which co-operation is possible. For today we all know that many who are in the same communion mean quite different things when they speak of the spiritual life, while conversely, thank Heaven, often in a communion which uses another vernacular may be found those who are practicing the Eternal Gospel. With those, therefore, in spite of difference of accent, full communion is possible and must be established. This is the task of a creative anthropology.

A church so constructed would have to be on a largely volunteer and almost-poverty basis—for what community could pay for five experts in one church? It would have to

[5] See John Hoyland's account of religious grouping for silent worship in *Digging for a New England*; and Dimond's, *The Psychology of the Methodist Revival*.

[217]

take all it could from modern education and from ancient practice. First and foremost it would find in both of these an agreement on the point that new members cannot be full members. Indeed the service offered must, it would seem, be threefold. To inquirers who simply want to hear if religion has a case to make, the sermon is open to all. Next must come catechumens, those who have come into training. Thirdly, there are those who have become full members. Full members would form a real *Oikos*, a union round a common Focus. As this is then a life of unlimited liability among such full members, the morality of such a group would be that of the Law of Equity. They would always arbitrate their differences between themselves; they would form a Co-operative embracing all their members; they would require nothing less than Sacramental marriage among all their members; their word would always be their bond; their sense of the Eternal Life would make death for them only an emergence and they would be constantly aware of those of their fellowship who had attained that freedom.

Such might be the beginning of that Tertiary Order in modern terms for which thinkers such as Douglas Steere have asked. It need not start large. Indeed it would be good that the church should always be so small that unless you came early you could not get in—or at least have the luxury of a seat. From such an Order, living the life of Equity, there might emerge those spiritual geniuses who could live the Law of Love and become the ambassadors of mankind. Genius cannot be created, but, as we know from all the great schools of art, if there are such schools the genius can then have the training which will make his supreme gift flower. If he does not get that teaching, too often his gift becomes distorted, spoiled by idiosyncrasy or indulgence.

[218]

And in the further extension of this pattern we are still only following the educative experience of mankind. All education tends to form into three levels. The first is that of the student. Of such would be those church members learning to practice fully the Law of Equity and to live in these groups which practice, at least internally, unlimited liability. The second is that of the master or fellow of the college, and of such would be these fivefold groupings of teaching experts, who are solely dedicated to the ministry in the various aspects of teaching the student body. The third consists of the doctor and of such would be those who are born with the high vocation so that with training they may be able to fulfill the Law of Love. The student is in Purgation: those in Equity who have become full members are in that fellowship which is called Proficiency, i.e., when a man or woman may openly profess that he or she has mastered the art of living as far as they and their comrades are concerned. The Doctorate is, as the word shows, the title and station of those who can go out and teach the world. Theirs is the contemporary apostolate. There is no task more important for the ministry than to pick these out from the students and train them for their world-wide task. The service done to those in studentship should be one that would solve the psychiatric problem. Here would be achieved that preventive and remedial work which the Church has let fall into the hands of the medical psychiatrist. It does not underrate his services to say that his standpoint cannot look beyond returning men to the norm and average. When we consider that genius, and especially spiritual genius, often in its metamorphic phase looks to an untrained eye as though it were not seeking a higher integration but failing to make the average, it is plain how much has been lost to religion by leaving all cases of mental

[219]

strain to be reduced by medical methods rather than sustained and composed by spiritual powers. Indeed we may venture to wonder whether in our mental institutions there may not be some, who debarred from the normal reaction and offered otherwise only confinement, had no choice but to be confined. No one who has studied that fascinating series of pictures called the "Authentic Likeness of the Saint" but can see clearly the truth of Professor Robert Thouless' contention that the saint and the mystic are very frequently made to achieve heroic virtue by first having to face, overcome and harmonize an endocrine disbalance which otherwise would have rendered them unfit for any normal living. Once that balance was achieved, so powerful were the opposites which had been brought into partnership, that the character became one to which the word "superhuman" is no misnomer.

Once this essential work of psychiatry is achieved, in its two aspects of raising those who have fallen into mental disorder and sending on to new heights those who have the vocation never to be able to be content with comfort, the cell or church can also go on to its second service to mankind, to the demonstration of how a free religious community living in Equity can give to the world a life-size model and working demonstration of an economy—and its necessary psychological background—which would if practiced by others solve our economic problems and class tensions.

The third service is, of course, to recruit and train for the "Doctorate" those men who can be the users of apt force. From these could come that combination of the old missionary and the new anthropologist. The zeal of the one combined with the tolerant respect and insight of the other could produce that type of man and those mobilized groups of men who could be the nuclear civil service of mankind, the apostolate of a new society.

I have now attempted to state in briefest terms the essentials of the Everlasting Gospel, the Perennial Philosophy. It teaches, I believe, the possibility and the necessity of man's union with himself, with his fellows and with the Eternal Life Itself, of which the visible Universe is but a manifestation. It declares that this world is a place for the development of the soul, for the emergence of a complete consciousness.

I have attempted to show that the task of man is to keep that knowledge, "In knowledge of Whom Standeth our eternal life," explicit. As man has to grow in "detached consciousness" there is a danger that, freed from instinct and given freedom, he may use his freedom not to give a larger meaning than instinct could provide, but a smaller, engrossment with his ego. Therefore he must continually make a balanced advance. Every insight into the outer world must be balanced by an equally enlarged knowledge of his true and full nature. Further, as that knowledge of the outer world grows in its sense of Time and, with that, in its knowledge of causality this will lead to the rise of the concept of Law. Therefore, as man forms notions of the outer Lawful-ness of events, he must realize the principle of Law running through his own inner life. He must find a Moral Law which is just as objective, as the laws which he perceives in the physical realm. This inner law should perhaps be better called psychological law rather than moral law.

We see that man has in the times in which we have been able to trace his psychological history with any clearness, time and again fallen away from the inner law, seduced by an unbalanced fascination with the outer law.

I have attempted to show how he has been recovered from these aberrations and how, therefore, Redemption is an actual part of human history.

Coming to the Christian Emphases: I have in the second part of this essay attempted to show five elements. First, there has been a brief sketch to show how Christendom did in actual fact go far to re-create that fourfold society which can balance psychological knowledge with physical powers. Secondly, I have sketched the development of that progressive social experimentation which in the religious houses during some one thousand years tried to work out new, more creative patterns of social living for those prepared to undertake avowed intentional co-operation. I have tried to show how and why these experiments became arrested and failed very largely at the time that the whole pattern of Christendom shrank and collapsed. Thirdly, I have tried to show the specific pattern of thought—the doctrine of the Redemptive Son and the Sanctifying Holy Ghost which gave Christianity its specific emphasis. Redemption is a recreative power which facing failure and wrongdoing yet maintains that salvage is always possible because the highest will always give himself for the lowest if the lowest will accept the loan; Sanctification is a progressively creative power which maintains that there is no limit to which the soul of man may not rise if it will but give itself to the Limitless. For Time is not an illusion or a trap for the soul which desires to know and be inspired by the perfect Wisdom—on the contrary, though how it may be remains a mystery of faith until faith turns into sight with Union, Time can be part of Eternity and the process here is of value to the Perfect Fact which at present we have to

[222]

imagine as being elsewhere. Fourthly, I have sketched even more briefly those specific spiritual exercises whereby, out of the number used by practitioners of the Eternal Gospel, Christians have won to the sense of Union and made that change of conduct into character and of character into consciousness, which is the soul's deliberate and conscious evolution in consciousness. Finally, I have ventured to indicate to what social pattern for mankind this Gospel and its methods would point.

I am certainly not unaware of the temerity of this effort. But I cannot doubt that in Christianity the Law of Charity has been recognized as that which rules all our relationships. It is under the protection of that Law that I would make my appeal to you that you would overlook the many ignorances which this essay will have revealed. Look upon what I have ventured to offer as the questions of an outsider deeply concerned and needing an answer in order to live better, and of one keenly aware that in religion and in it alone, as a growing and fresh source of truth and living experience, the future not merely of man's happiness but of his very existence depends.

APPENDIX

A hypothesis, in terms of the Eternal Gospel, of the theological dogmas of Original Sin, Predestination, Redemption and Eternal Death.

The doctrine of Original Sin as held by Orthodox Christianity is a particular rendering of the more widely spread and more comprehensive doctrine of karma. This is expressed most succinctly in the initial phrase of the *Dhammapada*, "All that we are is what we have thought." Such a conception is alien only to a materialistic philosophy. Our thought today is changing from epiphenomenalism to epinoumenalism. If, then, mind results in matter, and not matter in mind, we should expect that physique is a consequence of a causative psyche. Further, as we now have knowledge of our consciousness being far more extensive and profound than our self-consciousness, and of that deeper consciousness having control over the growth of the physique, we can see why, though we may have no surface knowledge of our responsibility of being what we are, we can be responsible. Because a man has forgotten an act, that certainly does not prove that he did not commit it. Because my surface self-conscious mind cannot directly affect matter, that does not mean that there is no type of consciousness which can.

I must then look upon physique as only the most ingrained and heavily-precipitated of habits, as, indeed, I must regard all matter as only the most rigorously confined form of mind.[1] Further, if I am to free myself from such habits as prove themselves to be mistaken, I must first accept the fact that I have so involved myself (and so can release myself) and then set

[1] See Von Hügel's *Eternal Life*.

[225]

about unwinding the coil of circumstance. From intellectual conviction I must go on to voluntary resolution: thence to re-training my habits (acts and speech), at the same time altering my occupations whenever they conflict with my new knowledge. I must also practice those mental exercises which keep me in decisive touch with my deeper mind.

The doctrine of Original Sin is thus seen in its pragmatic functionalism. It is not a metaphysical attempt to solve the problem of Evil. It is part of the minimum working hypothesis required to explain to each individual why he must accept responsibility for conditions for which he does not feel responsible, and how, if he so accepts—and only if he will so accept—he may become free and bring freedom to others. Original Sin requires, therefore, the acceptance of an idea of pre-existence. The notion of descent from Adam involving all his sons in his guilt was too physiological a way of trying to state the situation. Pre-incarnation is merely an over-vivid illustration attempting to make the same idea clear to ordinary minds. The Christian Church, after Chalcedon, condemned all metempsychosis, attaching itself forever to the inadequately narrow cosmology of Jewish apocalypticism. Hence, in its thinking, the Church was forced back on the doctrine of Predestination. Having to accept the fact that some men were in this life obviously unable, through physical and mental obstacles, to "work out their salvation," and debarred both from saying that such men before their birth made such obstacles and merited such handicaps and also after death could continue striving to remove them, the Church chose the only other alternative. This was bad: for that alternative is that God being above Moral Law can and does condemn men to lives which must end in destruction. This alternative had bad results, but not wholly bad. The doctrine of Predestination which drives the bad to a careless or desperate despair can keep the good from pride by teaching that all grace is primarily prevenient. Yet here, too, the doctrine can prove dangerously inadequate. For the good, while maintaining there is nothing good in themselves, may not only preen themselves on being selected for Salvation regardless of their efforts, but they may come to hold that any such effort on their part would be presumptuously otiose.

Modern biology, with its knowledge of genetic heredity and the "field" concepts of growth,[2] modern psychology with its research into the subconscious and the subconscious control over the physique, both suggest that religion may fruitfully rethink the dogmas of Original Sin and Predestination. The attempt must be to restate in modern working terms the facts which these dogmas rendered in ancient phrases. The attitude of those who would study religion today must be an extension of Lord Morley's phrase: "We will not denounce you: we will explain you." We certainly will not denounce: we will attempt to reinterpret.

This reinterpretation requires, I venture to believe, a combining of the dogma of Redemption with that of Original Sin. For if we have all failed somewhat before we came into the present body (which is partly a record of such failures) and such failures were once free mistakes (cf. "instinct as fossilized reason"), two further things are possible. There could be a stock, stem or phylum of Life which from the beginning never failed. At every level, however rudimentary, it did exercise to that full its capacity for creative acceptance and never shrank back into rejection and self-insulation. Hence it would be radically free: Its physique would in no wise thwart its wish to act without restraint: It would never be ignorant of its real relationship to all its fellows and to the Eternal Life. Hence it would not only be mobilized wholly to serve others—they could come to salvation through it. For this power, to transcend the illusory but stubborn limitations of physique-personality, would make it possible for it to transfuse its vitality-consciousness into any who would accept this unique service (cf. "As many as received him, to them gave he power to become the sons of God [John 1:12]). This, too, is the

2 See Hans Spemann's *Organizer*.

Vedanta doctrine of the Avatar, the Mahayana doctrine of the Bodhisattva and possibly the Taoist theory of the "Immortal."

This estimate of Redemption is borne out by such classic studies in Evolution as resulted in the conclusion that not only is "man the fetalization of the ape," i.e., man does manage to retain until adulthood a childlike freedom even of physique which the ape loses long before adolescence and indeed in some respects before birth—but also "the dog is the fetalization of the wolf." It has been convincingly shown by comparison of the fetal skull and forelimbs of the wolf with those of the full-grown spaniels and other highly developed dogs, that these, in their association with man, have been able to abandon their fatal specialization as carnivora parasitic on the ruminants, and actually to go far to recover that generalized physique which is the rightful accompaniment of a regeneralized psyche—a psyche which has recovered that general interest which is the common basis of friendliness and educability.

If such a change can take place in a few thousand years of casual acquaintance with not very lofty men—undoing millions of years of predatory specialization—we cannot be sure that the whole of the rigidity may not be re-suppled, and the paw—which every intelligent dog strives so hard to use as a hand—may, generation by generation, recover its stunted digits.[3]

Quite another example of the Redemptive development may be found, not in what the saved experience but in the savior's own growth. The present Studies in Precognition in Britain and at Duke University, are increasingly difficult to dismiss. They present, however, serious philosophic difficulties. The theory that would best accommodate them, makes nevertheless remarkable contribution to our exploration of human capacity. It would seem that most of our acts that we consider

[3] This recovery of generalized form once it has become specialized is generally deemed by anatomists to be impossible but there seem a few cases on record, e.g., the resumption of a scale form from a feather specialization.

free are really the result of conditioned reflexes. But every now and then we do hold up the impulse to act unreflectively. This *contra agere* breaks the entail. We are then free to act with real freedom. And as that is real freedom, and not merely a feeling, that real act brings into the Space-Time continuum something which has never been there before, something radically new. Every such really free act is then in the strict sense of the word a creative act and so actually reverses to that degree the entropic process otherwise inevitable to all natural things. Further, each such act gives, as we may say, a "bonus" of two more free acts: until the person, by these persistent acts of enlightened liberation, becomes totally free—every act he performs is wholly creative.

This explanation of Precognition would see it (in accord with the new physics) as evidence of a capacity to gain such detachment from physiological immediacy that in the end Time can be seen—as physics knows it to be—as an aspect of Space, and not, as we commonly experience it, as something apart from Space. The more we are detached from the body, the easier it is to have such glimpses; as when in a plane, the higher its elevation, the farther we can see along rail tracks at ground level.

The savior, therefore, not only can, by his fearless and self-less devotion, win the saving devotion of the creature, who cannot unsnarl himself. But the savior himself enters into a new knowledge (gnosis) of the universe. He is not merely being gallantly kind, touched with a heartbroken compassion for suffering. He actually experiences the universe as it actually is and, so seeing, he is able to set others in the way of that seeing, which, being enlightenment, must bring liberation.

Standing somewhat outside these dogmas which we have been discussing is what we may call the residual dogma of damnation. What is the ultimate fate of the soul which will continue to defy God? Christian theology, using here a psychology which made man's nature simply dual (an animal body and a spirit eternal, because a spark of God's spirit),

[229]

involved itself in grave difficulty. Had it developed the tripartite psychology used tentatively by St. Paul, it could have preserved the two values it desired to protect and yet have guarded against degrading its concept of Divine Nature. The two values are the immense importance of this life and of human free will. The tripartite psychology could solve the two demands (that the choice made in this life should be of eternal significance and that the soul is really free to refuse the Divine offer of Eternal Life) and yet preserve the Holiness of God from the blasphemous aspersion that He is capable of tormenting a soul forever. For the tripartite psychology allows that the spirit in man, the *scintilla Dei*, is irrevocably eternal, being of God's spirit. It also recognizes an animal nature which is identified with the body and which perishes with it or soon after (cf. the electrical physiological "field" of modern biophysics and the Ka of Egyptian metaphysics). But between these two it detects a middle element, the detached consciousness—the *ahamkara* ("the conceit of individuality") of the Sankhya, the system of Sanskrit psychology which is basic to Buddhism. It is the existence of this consciousness-element which gives the whole meaning to life. For here, with this factor, is played out the drama of real free will, of which this world is the stage. Without this element, life can never be fully real. For either—as in materialistic epochs—we describe ourselves as animals and death is then our complete frustration, we are merely bubbles; or, on the other hand, in strictly "Idealistic" ages, we see ourselves as unaffected eternal spirits, and then the world and this life is less than a show—it is merely a shadow on a shadow. But if we are tripartite creatures, then this central term of the detached consciousness—the jiva—can in this life choose to be "born again," can choose to detach itself from its vehicle of the animal life before that body falls to pieces and attach itself to the divine spark, the Atman, which, until death, will solicit from it this saving union.

The detached consciousness is then conditionally immortal

and this life gains its intended dignity when we see it as that brief opportunity during which we can make this essential contact and achieve this identification. If the detached consciousness (the "soul" in distinction from the "spirit") fails in this life—or fails to the limit of Time (for it is more than possible that Time exists beyond the sensory world) then, once it has lost all vehicle and container and yet not achieved union with the Timeless, it has no purchase or form of any kind, it might well be unable to sustain itself and so dissolve.

The Spirit, the Atman, would return to God, the Eternal, and the whole incident would have been in vain, frustrated by the soul's refusal to avail itself of the opportunity of becoming one with the Eternal. The Atman would have gained nothing and lost nothing. It can give: it cannot gain. The experience which could have been of value was the temporal experience of the soul. The saved soul would have brought this up to the Eternal Life. There is, then, irremediable loss, not Eternal Pain. Evil and its profound wish for separateness has ended as it must end in annihilation, nothingness. A unique opportunity has been lost. That which is unconditionally Eternal— the *scintilla Dei*—cannot perish or suffer. That which is conditionally eternal can suffer and so can perish. The destruction is complete as far as it concerns a destructable thing. The loss is utter, in so far as a conditionally eternal creature has chosen to miscarry and to be nothing rather than to be part of All. The Atman would have no specific memory of that particular life, because the process was never completed. As with a photographic plate which was never developed before the camera fell to pieces and the plate was exposed to the light, so the specific picture made by the Eternal Light, coming through a particular camera and lens of consciousness (the human bodymind) would be obliterated at death (or whenever the biophysical body-precipitating field is dissolved)[4] The dust would

[4] It should be observed that the great psychological analysis derived from the Vedas by Sankara perceives in man not merely a triple nature but one that is Fivefold: There is the body, the Physical

return to the dust, the *ahamkara* or psyche would dissipate, the Atman would return to God who gave it and be re-assimilated in Him. Justice would be done: the Second Death would be a real death, for the *ahamkara* would be as though it had never been: and mercy would not be outraged.

Conversely, the soul that hears the call, accepts the divine offer of Union and enters on that path, would carry its consciousness up with it, and the Eternal is enriched with that aspect, however minute, of completed Time. This final point, as has been said in the body of the book, makes the Temporal Universe valuable in itself, not merely as a place of trial and redemption but also as a stage of sanctification and creation. The saved are permitted to bring a contribution, however small, to the bliss of All.

It is also important to notice in this difficult but important issue that the modernist Von Hügel, whose theological thought is increasingly influential, accepts the fact that the Second Death or Eternal Damnation is total loss of memory, and so, of course, of consciousness, as we know it. It is an important fact, which we should bear in mind, that—as research in anesthetics and hypnotism shows—total loss of memory, by removing any recollection of the past and so also any power to apprehend the future, means the disappearance of pain as

---

Sheath, or core: around that and precipitating it is the Vital Sheath, which no doubt can now be identified with the electrical field of the body: around this second Sheath is the third, Manas, the mind that uses the senses and has the sense of the "I, the me and the mine" and perceiving only the phenomenal world identifies itself with that and its own body. There is a fourth Sheath which embraces these inner sheathes, and this fourth is the pure intellect—above the ratiocinative analytic reason-mind—but still "desiring to be the doer" and so still self-willed. Above that is the fifth, the Eternal Spirit and Spark of God in man, "the Atman who is Brahman." It is evident that in this Fivefold analysis of consciousness, that the factor that can become eternal, by dissociating itself with what St. Paul calls the carnal mind, is the fourth Sheath, the Sheath of Intellect which Sankara says shines with the light which the Atman (God Imminent: the *scintilla Dei*) casts directly upon it.

[232]

we experience it, e.g., experiments with nitrous oxide. A being who has lost all memory—not merely of the middle-distance past but of everything up to that tenth of a second, within which span of "specious present" consciousness cannot be experienced—is completely anesthetized and unaware of being anywhere or anyone in particular. And should that loss of sense extend into the subconscious, then the continuity of subconscious experience being itself lost, the person would be dissolved and it is hard to see where there would remain anything round which a reassemblage could take place. If, however, a latent sub-suffering strain of consciousness remains, then that could once again be roused and hell would only be an extended purgatory. If, on the other hand, the will remains eternally in revolt against God then this can only point to a Manichaean Dualism which Christianity utterly rejected. It is clear that because Aquinas accepted a dualistic instead of a tripartite concept of human nature, he cannot reconcile the mutual contradiction of the two facts which he accepts: That the soul is indeed the spark of God Himself, the Atman is Brahman and that such a soul, if eternally damned, does not suffer a second death but an eternal life of torment. Quite apart from the fact that eternal life in pain cannot be called death—a fact stressed by the Swiss theologian Dr. Petavel fifty years ago—Aquinas is forced into a further difficulty, one might almost say absurdity. For he teaches that God's actual Nature never departs from the damned, for that Nature, being essentially Eternal cannot be destroyed. But, quite apart from the fact that this statement denies another principal dogma concerning God's Nature, that that Nature is impassible for being outside Time or accident it is incapable of suffering. Aquinas involves himself in the contradiction that God damns part of Himself and submits to an Eternal frustration of His intention and design. As He is incapable of eternal fission—being the One—or frustration—being the Almighty—the argument falls. Failure can only be temporal. An actual state of Eternal frustration is a philosophic contradiction, a real ab-

[233]

surdity. Later theologians have tried to save this situation of Roman Orthodoxy by urging that the soul is in hell through a constant and deliberate act of the will and so eternally chooses its separation from God, which state of the will is hell. But this, again, makes eternal the individual will as an alien force against God and this can only be maintained by a Manichaean Dualism. Surely the difficulty arises because we confuse the age-long (*aevum*) with the eternal (*aeternitas*). It is clear that God has given man everything but the understanding of, and power over, Time. It alone is for him irreversible, while for God this limitation does not exist. Here is the secret of Redemption, for God can annihilate the past. Here is the meaning in the creation myth with its sequel in a Fall, that God let man eat of the forbidden tree of the knowledge of Good and Evil but not of the tree of Life—or Eternal Life. It is clear that God permits us terrible powers, for the time being, but the time being is even to our vision, ridiculously small. Most human monsters have only been actively destructive for some twenty or thirty years. They then die and their fame often fades as quickly as their wicked policies are swept away. Beside astronomical time, they are not even Ephemerida; beside the geological record they are still only creatures of a moment; beside the growth of a Sequoia they are mere incidents.

The above tentative suggestions are not put forward as contributions to Theodicy. They are only advanced to question and perhaps help to check that type of dogmatic ratiocination which, starting with an antinomy ill-defined in an ankylosed tradition, attempts to force a premature synthesis and so fails to preserve either of the opposed or balanced values, which it proposed to reconcile but which in actual fact it degrades.